INTERNATIONAL CENTRE FOR MECHANICAL SCIENCES

COURSES AND LECTURES - No. 166

TOBY BERGER
CORNELL UNIVERSITY
ITHACA, NEW YORK

AND

LEE D. DAVISSON
UNIVERSITY OF SOUTHERN CALIFORNIA
LOS ANGELES, CALIFORNIA

ADVANCES IN SOURCE CODING

UDINE 1975

SPRINGER-VERLAG WIEN GMBH

Originally published by Springer-Verlag Wien New York in 1975

ISBN 978-3-211-81302-7 ISBN 978-3-7091-2928-9 (eBook)
DOI 10.1007/978-3-7091-2928-9

RATE DISTORTION THEORY AND DATA COMPRESSION

TOBY BERGER
School of Electrical Engineering
Cornell University, Ithaca, New York

PREFACE

I am grateful to CISM and to Prof. Giuseppe Longo for the opportunity to lecture about rate distortion theory research during the 1973 CISM summer school session. Rate distortion theory is currently the most vital area of probabilistic information theory, affording significantly increased insight and understanding about data compression mechanisms in both man-made and natural information processing systems. The lectures that follow are intended to convey an appreciation for the important results that have been obtained to date and the challenging problems that remain to be resolved in this rapidly evolving branch of information theory. The international composition of the CISM summer school attendees affords a unique opportunity to attempt to stimulate subsequent contributions to the theory from many nations. It is my hope that the lectures which follow capitalize successfully on this promising opportunity.

T. Berger

LECTURE 1

Rate Distortion Theory: An Introduction

In this introductory lecture we present the rudiments of rate distortion theory, the branch of information theory that treats data compression problems. The rate distortion function is defined and a powerful iterative algorithm for calculating it is described. Shannon's source coding theorems are stated and heuristically discussed.

Shannon's celebrated coding theorem states that a source of entropy rate H can be transmitted reliably over any channel of capacity $C > H$. This theorem also has a converse devoted to the frequently encountered situation in which the entropy rate of the source exceeds the capacity of the channel. Said converse states that not all the source data can be recovered reliably when $H > C$ [1].

Since it is always desirable to recover all the data correctly, one can reduce H either by

(a) slowing down the rate of production of source letters, or

(b) encoding the letters more slowly than they are being produced.

However, (a) often is impossible because the source rate is not under the communication system designer's control, and (b) often is impossible both because the data becomes stale, or perhaps even useless, because of long coding delays and because extensive buffering memory is needed.

If H cannot be lowered, then the only other remedy is to increase C. This, however, is usually very expensive in practice. We shall assume in all that follows that H already has been lowered and that C already has been raised as much as is practically possible but the situation $H > C$ nonetheless continues to prevail. (This is always true in the important case of analog sources because their absolute entropy H is infinite whereas the C of any physical channel is finite). In such a situation it is reasonable to attempt to preserve those aspects of the source data that are the most crucial to the application at hand. That is, the communication system should be configured to reconstruct the source data at the channel output with minimum possible *distortion* subject to the requirement that the rate of transmission of information cannot exceed the channel capacity. Obviously, there is a tradeoff between the rate at which information is provided about the output of a data source and the fidelity with which said output can be reconstructed on the basis of this information. The mathematical discipline that treats this tradeoff from the viewpoint of information theory is known as rate distortion theory.

A graphical sketch of a typical rate-distortion tradeoff is shown in Figure 1. If the rate R at which

Figure 1. A Typical Rate-Distortion Tradeoff

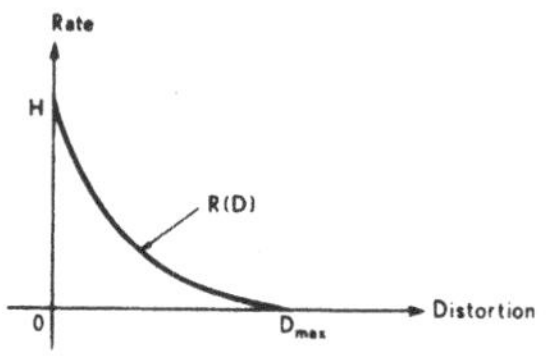

information can be provided about the source output exceeds H, then no distortion need result. As R decreases from H towards 0, the minimum attainable distortion steadily increases from 0 to the value D_{max} associated with the best guess one can make in the total absence of any information about the source outputs. Curves that quantify such tradeoffs aptly have been termed rate distortion functions by Shannon [2].

The crucial property that a satisfactorily defined rate distortion function R(D) possesses is the following:

(*) "It is possible to compress the data rate from H down to any R > R(D) and still be able to recover the original source outputs with an average distortion not exceeding D. Conversely, if the compressed data rate R satisfies R < R(D), then it is not possible to recover the original source data from the compressed version with an average distortion of D or less".

An R(D) curve that posssesses the above property clearly functions as an extension, or generalization, of the concept of entropy. Just as H is the minimum data rate (channel capacity) needed to transmit the source data with zero average distortion, R(D) is the minimum data rate (channel capacity) needed to transmit the data with average distortion D.

Omnis rate distortion theory in tres partes divisa est.

(i) Definition, calculation and bounding of R(D) curves for various data sources and distortion measures.

(ii) Proving of coding theorems which establish that said R(D) curves do indeed specify the absolute limit on the rate vs. distortion tradeoff in the sense of (*).

(iii) Designing and analyzing practical communication systems whose performances closely approach the ideal limit set by R(D).

We shall begin by defining R(D) for the case of a memoryless source and a context-free distortion measure. This is the simplest case from the mathematical viewpoint, but unfortunately it is the least interesting case from the viewpoint of practical applications. The memoryless nature of the source limits the extent to which the data rate can be compressed without severe distortion being incurred. Moreover, because of the assumption that even isolated errors cannot be corrected from contextual considerations, the ability to compress the data rate substantially without incurring intolerable distortion is further curtailed. Accordingly, we subsequently shall extend the development to situations in which the source has memory and/or the fidelity criterion has context-dependence.

A discrete memoryless source generates a sequence $\{X_1, X_2, \ldots\}$ of independent identically distributed random variables (i.i.d. r.v.'s). Each X_i assumes a value in the finite set $A = \{a_1, \ldots, a_M\}$ called the source alphabet. The probability that $X_i = a_j$ will be denoted by $P(a_j)$. This probability does not depend on i because the source outputs are identically distributed. Let $\underline{X} = (X_1, \ldots, X_n)$ denote a random vector of n successive source outputs, and let $\underline{x} = (x_1, \ldots, x_n) \in A^n$ denote a value that $\underline{X}$ can assume. Then the probability $P_n(\underline{x})$ that $\underline{X}$ assumes the value $\underline{x}$ is given by

$$P_n(\underline{x}) = \prod_{t=1}^{n} P(x_t)$$

because the source has been assumed to be memoryless.

A communication system is to be built that will attempt to convey the sequence of source outputs to an interested user, as depicted in Figure 2.

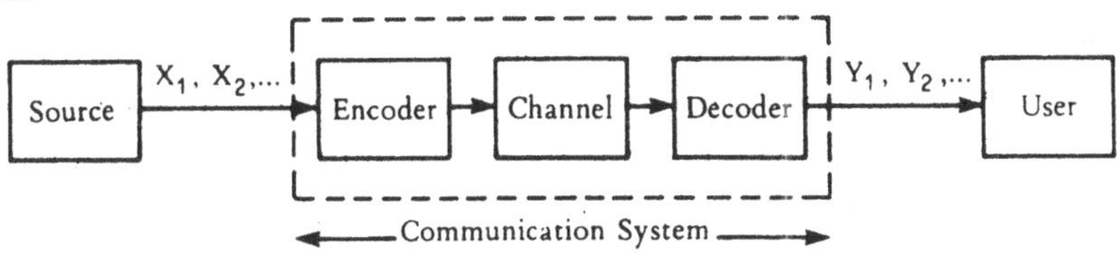

Figure 2. A Communication System Linking Source to User

Let $Y_1, Y_2, \ldots$ denote the sequence of letters received by the user. In general, the Y_i assume values in an alphabet $B = \{b_1, \ldots b_N\}$ of letters that may differ both in value and in cardinality from the source alphabet A, although A = B in most applications.

In order to quantify the rate-distortion tradeoff, we must have a means of specifying the distortion that results when $X_i = a_j$ and $Y_i = b_k$. We shall assume that there is given for this purpose a so-called distortion measure ρ: $A\times B \to [0,\infty]$. That is, $\rho(a_j, b_k)$ is the penalty, loss, cost, or distortion that results when the source produces a_j and the system delivers b_k to the user. Moreover, we shall assume that the distortion $\rho_n(\underline{x},\underline{y})$ that results when a vector $\underline{x} \in A^n$ of n successive source letters is represented to the user as $\underline{y} \in B^n$ is of the form

$$\rho_n(\underline{x},\underline{y}) = n^{-1} \sum_{t=1}^{n} \rho(x_t, y_t).$$

A family $\{\rho_n, 1 \leqslant n < \infty\}$ of such vector distortion measures will be referred to as a single-letter, or memoryless, fidelity criterion because the penalty charged for each error the system makes does not depend on the overall context in which the error occurs.

Example:

$$A = B = \{0,1\}$$

$$\rho(0,0) = \rho(1,1) = 0$$

$$\rho(0,1) = \alpha, \ \rho(1,0) = \beta$$

Then $$\rho_3(010,001) = \frac{1}{3}(0 + \alpha + \beta) = \frac{\alpha+\beta}{3}$$

Each communication system linking source to user in Figure 2 may be fully described for statistical purposes by specifying for each $j \in \{1, ..., M\}$ and $k \in \{1, ..., N\}$ the probability $Q_{k/j}$ that a typical system output Y will be equal to b_k given that the corresponding input X equals a_j. Contracting notation from $P(a_j)$ to P_j and from $\rho(a_j, b_k)$ to ρ_{jk}, we may associate with each system $Q = (Q_{k/j})$ two functions of extreme importance, namely

$$I(Q) = \sum_{j=1}^{M} \sum_{k=1}^{N} P_j Q_{k/j} \log\left(\frac{Q_{k/j}}{Q_k}\right), \text{ where } Q_k = \sum_j P_j Q_{k/j}$$

and

$$d(Q) = \sum_{j,k} P_j Q_{k/j} \rho_{jk}$$

I(Q) is the average mutual information between source and user for the system Q, and d(Q) is the average distortion with which the source outputs are reproduced for the user by system Q. For situations in which both the source and the fidelity criterion are memoryless, Shannon [2] has defined the rate distortion function R(D) as follows

$$\boxed{R(D) = \min_{Q : d(Q) \leq D} I(Q)}$$

That is, we restrict our attention to those systems Q whose average distortion d(Q) does not exceed a specified level D of tolerable average distortion, and then we search among this set of Q's for the one with the minimum value of I(Q). We minimize rather than maximize I(Q) because we wish to supply as little information as possible about the source outputs provided, of course, that we preserve the data with the required fidelity D. In physical terms, we wish to compress the rate of transmission of information to the lowest value consistent with the requirement that the average distortion may not exceed D.

Remark: An equivalent definition of the critical curve in the (R,D)-plane in which R is the independent and D the dependent variable is

$$D(R) = \min_{Q : I(Q) \leq R} d(Q) .$$

This so-called "distortion rate function" concept is more intuitively satisfying because average distortion gets minimized rather than average mutual information. Moreover, the constraint $I(Q) \leq R$ has the physical significance that the compressed data rate cannot exceed a specified value which in practice would be the capacity C of the channel in the communication link of Figure 2. It is probably unfortunate that Shannon chose to employ the R(D) rather than the D(R) approach.

LECTURE 2.

Computation of R(D)

The definition of R(D) that we have given thus far is not imbued with any physical significance because we have not yet proved the crucial source-coding theorem and converse for R(D) so defined. We shall temporarily ignore this fact and concentrate instead on procedures for calculating R(D) curves in practical examples. Until recently, it was possible to find R(D) only in special examples involving either small M and N or $\{P_j\}$ and (ρ_{jk}) with special symmetry properties. A recent advance by Blahut, however, permits rapid and accurate calculation of R(D) in the general case [3].

The problem of computing R(D) is one in convex programming. The mutual information functional I(Q) is convex ∪ in Q (Homework). It must be minimized subject to the linear equality and inequality constraints

$$\sum_{k=1}^{N} Q_{k/j} = 1 \quad , \quad 1 \leqslant j \leqslant M$$

$$\sum_{j,k} P_j Q_{k/j} \rho_{jk} \leqslant D$$

and $Q_{k/j} \geqslant 0$. Accordingly, the Kuhn-Tucker theorem can be applied to determine necessary and sufficient conditions that characterize the optimum transition probability assignment. Said conditions assume the following form:

Theorem 1. - Fix $s \in [-\infty, 0]$. Then there is a line of slope s tangent to the R(D) curve at the point (d(Q), I(Q)) if and only if there exists a probability vector $\{Q_k, 1 \leqslant k \leqslant N\}$ such that

(i) $$Q_{k/j} = \lambda_j Q_k e^{s\rho_{jk}} \quad , \quad \text{where } \lambda_j = \Big(\sum_k Q_k e^{s\rho_{jk}}\Big)^{-1} ,$$

and

(ii) $$C_k \triangleq \sum_j \lambda_j P_j e^{s\rho_{jk}} \begin{cases} = 1 \text{ for all } k \text{ such that } Q_k > 0 \\ \leqslant 1 \text{ for all } k \text{ such that } Q_k = 0 \end{cases}$$

Proof: Straightforward application of the Kuhn-Tucker theorem.

The theorem above shows that the R(D) curve can be generated parametrically by choosing different values of $s \in [-\infty, 0]$ and then determining the corresponding optimum $\{Q_k\}$ vectors.

The following theorem describes Blahut's iterative algorithm which converges to the optimum $\{Q_k\}$ vector, and hence yields the optimum system of transition probabilities $Q_{k/j}$ associated with a particular value s of the slope parameter.

Theorem 2. - Given $s \in [-\infty, 0]$, choose any probability vector Q_k^o, $1 \leq k \leq N$ with strictly positive components $Q_k^o > 0$. Define

$$Q_k^{r+1} = c_k^r Q_k^r$$

where

$$c_k^r = \sum \lambda_j^r P_j e^{s\rho_{jk}} \quad \text{and} \quad \lambda_j^r = \left(\sum_k Q_k^r e^{s\rho_{jk}} \right)^{-1} .$$

Then $\{Q_k^r\}$ converges to the $\{Q_k\}$ that satisfies (i) and (ii) of theorem 1 as $r \to \infty$.

Proof: Lemma: $\log x \leq x-1$ (natural logarithm)

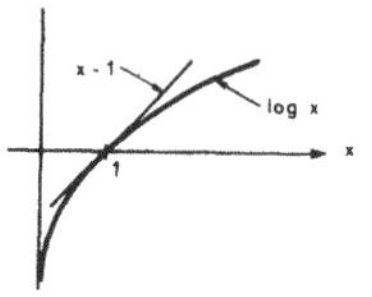

Proof of Lemma:

Since $\log(x)$ is convex $\cap$ and both $\log x$ and $x-1$ equal zero and have slope 1 at $x = 1$, the tangent line $x-1$ must lie above the curve $\log x$ for all x. This completes the proof of the lemma. ($\log x \leq x - 1$ is often called the fundamental inequality).

Corollary of Lemma: $\log y \geq 1 - 1/y$. (Proof omitted.)

To prove the theorem we consider the functional $V(Q) = I(Q) - sd(Q)$. The graphical significance of V(Q) is shown in Figure 3. It is the R-axis intercept of a

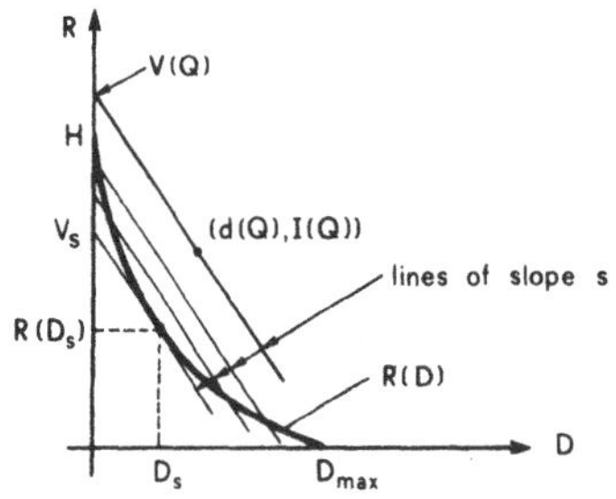

Figure 3. Graphical Description of V(Q)

line of slope s through the point (d(Q), I(Q)) in the (R,D)- plane. For any Q the point (d(Q), I(Q)) necessarily lies on or above the R(D) curve by definition of the latter. Since R(D) is convex ∪ (Homework), it follows that $V(Q) \geqslant V_s$, the R-axis intercept of the line of slope s that is tangent to R(D).

The Blahut iterative formula $Q_k^{r+1} = c_k^r Q_k^r$ can be thought of as the composition of two successive steps; namely starting from $\{Q_k^r\}$, we have

Step 1.

$$Q_{k/j}^{r+1} = \frac{Q_k^r e^{s\rho_{jk}}}{\sum_k Q_k^r e^{s\rho_{jk}}} = \lambda_j^r Q_k^r e^{s\rho_{jk}}$$

Step 2.

$$\begin{aligned} Q_k^{r+1} &= \sum_j P_j Q_{k/j}^{r+1} \\ &= \sum_j \lambda_j^r P_j Q_k^r e^{s\rho_{jk}} = c_k^r Q_k^r \end{aligned}$$

We proceed to show that $V(Q^r) \to V_s$ as $r \to \infty$, which in turn clearly implies from Figure 3 that $(d(Q^r), I(Q^r))$ converges to the point $(D_s, R(D_s))$ at which the slope of R(.) is s. Let us contract notation from $V(Q^r)$ to V^r. Then

$$\begin{aligned} V^{r+1} &= \sum_{j,k} P_j Q_{k/j}^{r+1} \log \frac{Q_{k/j}^{r+1}}{Q_k^{r+1}} - s \sum_{j,k} P_j Q_{k/j}^{r+1} \rho_{jk} \\ &= \sum_{j,k} P_j Q_{k/j}^{r+1} \log\left(\frac{\lambda_j^r Q_k^r e^{s\rho_{jk}}}{Q_k^{r+1}}\right) - \sum_{j,k} P_j Q_{k/j}^{r+1} \log\left(e^{s\rho_{jk}}\right) \\ &= \sum_j P_j \log(\lambda_j^r) + \sum_k Q_k^{r+1} \log\left(Q_k^r / Q_k^{r+1}\right) \end{aligned}$$

Hence, with the aid of the lemma we get

$$\begin{aligned} V^r - V^{r+1} &= \sum_{j,k} P_j Q_{k/j}^r \log\left(\frac{Q_{k/j}^r e^{-s\rho_{jk}}}{Q_k^r \lambda_j^r}\right) + \sum_k Q_k^{r+1} \log\left(\frac{Q_k^{r+1}}{Q_k^r}\right) \\ &\geqslant \sum_{j,k} P_j Q_{k/j}^r \left[1 - \frac{\lambda_j^r Q_k^r e^{s\rho_{jk}}}{Q_{k/j}^r}\right] + \sum_k Q_k^{r+1} \left(1 - \frac{Q_k^r}{Q_k^{r+1}}\right) \end{aligned}$$

$$= 1 - \sum_k Q_k^r \sum_j \lambda_j^r P_j e^{s\rho_{jk}} + 1 - \sum_k Q_k^r$$

$$= 1 - \sum_k Q_k^r c_k^r + 1 - 1 = 1 - \sum_k Q_k^{r+1} = 1 - 1 = 0.$$

This establishes that V is monotonic nonincreasing* in r and hence converges because it is bounded from below by V_s. It only remains to show that the value to which V^r converges is V_s rather than some higher value. This is argued by noting that equality must hold in the above argument at the convergence point which in turn requires that $Q_k^{r+1}/Q_k^r = c_k^r \to 1 \; \forall k$ such that $\lim_{r\to\infty} Q_k^r > 0$. That is, the first of the Kuhn-Tucker conditions must be satisfied at the convergence point. But the second one also must be satisfied there since, if $\lim_{r\to\infty} c_k^r > 1$ for any k, then convergence cannot occur because $0 < Q_k^{r+1} = c_k^r Q_k^r$. This completes the proof of the theorem and also completes Lecture 2.

* In fact, V^r is strictly decreasing whenever $V^r > V_s$. To see this, note that the inequality used to show the nonincreasing nature of V^r is strict unless $Q_k^{r+1} = Q_k^r \; \forall k$, i.e. unless $c_k^r = 1 \; \forall k$. But $c_k^r = 1 \; \forall k$ implies that Q_k^r is optimum and hence that $V^r = V_s$.

LECTURE 3.

The Lower Bound Theorem and Error Estimates for the Blahut Algorithm

We have just seen how Blahut's iterative algorithm provides a powerful tool for the computation of R(D) curves. The following rather remarkable theorem is most interesting in its own right and also provides a means for ascertaining when the Blahut iterations have progressed to the point that $(d(Q^r), I(Q^r))$ is within some specified ϵ of the R(D) curve.

Theorem 3.

$$R(D) = \max_{s \leqslant 0,\ \underline{\lambda} \in \Lambda_s} \left(sD + \sum_j P_j \log \lambda_j \right)$$

where

$$\Lambda_s = \left\{ \underline{\lambda} = (\lambda_1, \ldots, \lambda_n) : \lambda_j \geqslant 0 \ \forall j, \text{and} \quad C_k \triangleq \sum_j \lambda_j P_j e^{s\rho_{jk}} \leqslant 1 \ \forall k \right\}$$

Remark: This theorem gives a representation of R(D) in the form of a maximum of a different function in a different convex region. Hence, it permits lower bounds to R(D) to be generated easily just as the original definition permitted generation of upper bounds in the form of I(Q) for any D-admissible Q.

Proof: Choose any $s \leqslant 0$, any $\underline{\lambda} \in \Lambda_s$, and any Q such that $d(Q) \leqslant D$. Then

$$I(Q) - sD - \sum_j P_j \log \lambda_j$$

$$\overset{(1)}{\geqslant} I(Q) - sd(Q) - \sum_j P_j \log \lambda_j$$

$$= \sum_{j,k} P_j Q_{k/j} \log \left(\frac{Q_{k/j}}{\lambda_j Q_k e^{s\rho_{jk}}} \right)$$

$$\overset{(2)}{\geq} \sum_{j,k} P_j Q_{k/j}\left(1 - \frac{\lambda_j Q_k e^{s\rho_{jk}}}{Q_{k/j}}\right)$$

$$= 1 - \sum_k Q_k \sum_j \lambda_j P_j e^{s\rho_{jk}} = 1 - \sum_k Q_k C_k$$

$$\overset{(3)}{\geq} 1 - \sum_k Q_k = 1 - 1 = 0$$

[$\overset{(1)}{\geq}$ results from the conditions $s \leq O$ and $d(Q) \leq D$.
$\overset{(2)}{\geq}$ is the fundamental inequality
$\overset{(3)}{\geq}$ results from the fact that $\underline{\lambda} \in \Lambda_s$]

We have just shown that $(d(Q) \leq D) \Rightarrow (I(Q) \geq sD + \sum P_j \log \lambda_j$ for any $s \leq O$ and any $\underline{\lambda} \in \Lambda_s$). It follows that $(d(Q) \leq D) \Rightarrow (I(Q) \geq \max_{s \leq O, \underline{\lambda} \in \Lambda_s} sD + \sum_j P_j \log \lambda_j)$.

Accordingly

$$R(D) \triangleq \min_{Q : d(Q) \leq D} I(Q) \geq \max_{s \leq 0, \underline{\lambda} \in \Lambda_s} (sD + \sum_j P_j \log \lambda_j)$$

which establishes the advertized lower bound. That the reverse inequality also holds, and hence that the theorem is true, is established by recalling that the Q that solves the original R(D) problem must be of the form

$$Q_{k/j} = \lambda_j Q_k e^{s\rho_{jk}}$$

so that for this Q we have

$$R(D) = I(Q) = \sum_{j,k} P_j Q_{k/j} \log\left(\frac{Q_{k/j}}{Q_k}\right) = \sum_{j,k} P_j Q_{k/j} \log\left(\lambda_j e^{s\rho_{jk}}\right)$$

$$= s\sum_{j,k} P_j Q_{k/j}\rho_{jk} + \sum_j P_j \log \lambda_j$$

$$= sd(Q) + \sum_j P_j \log \lambda_j = sD + \sum_j P_j \log \lambda_j ,$$

since $d(Q) = D$ for the Q that solves the R(D) problem. Also, we know that $C_k \leq 1$ for this Q, so $\underline{\lambda} \in \Lambda_s$. Thus R(D) is of the form $sD + \sum_j P_j \log \lambda_j$ for some $s \leq O$ and some $\underline{\lambda} \in \Lambda_s$. Therefore

$$R(D) \leqslant \max_{s \leqslant 0,\, \lambda \in \Lambda_s} \; sD + \sum_j P_j \log \lambda_j$$

and the theorem is proved.

Let us return to step (r + 1) of the Blahut algorithm in which we defined

$$Q_{k/j}^{r+1} = \lambda_j^r Q_k^r e^{s\rho_{jk}} \quad \text{and} \quad Q_k^{r+1} = c_k^r Q_k^r$$

Let $d(Q^{r+1}) = D$. It then follows that

$$R(D) \leqslant I(Q^{r+1}) = \sum_{j,k} P_j Q_{k/j}^{r+1} \log \frac{Q_{k/j}^{r+1}}{Q_k^{r+1}}$$

$$= \sum_{j,k} P_j Q_{k/j}^{r+1} \log \frac{\lambda_j^r e^{s\rho_{jk}}}{C_k^r}$$

$$= s \sum_{j,k} P_j Q_{k/j}^{r+1} \rho_{jk} + \sum_j P_j \log \lambda_j^r - \sum_k Q_k^r \log (C_k^r) \sum_j \lambda_j^r P_j e^{s\rho_{jk}}$$

$$= sd(Q^{r+1}) + \sum_j P_j \log \lambda_j^r - \sum_k Q_k^r c_k^r \log C_k^r, \quad \text{or}$$

$$R(D) \leqslant sD + \sum_j P_j \log \lambda_j^r - \sum_k Q_k^r c_k^r \log c_k^r = R_U^r(D)$$

which is an upper bound to R(D) at the value of distortion associated with iteration r + 1. We can obtain a lower bound to R(D) at the same value of D with the help of Theorem 3 by defining

$$c_{max}^r = \max_k c_k^r = \max_k \sum_j \lambda_j^r P_j e^{s\rho_{jk}}$$

and then setting

$$\lambda_j' = \frac{\lambda_j^r}{c_{max}^r} .$$

It follows that

$$c_k' \triangleq \sum_j \lambda_j' P_j e^{s\rho_{jk}} = \frac{1}{c^r_{max}} \sum_j \lambda_j^r P_j e^{s\rho_{jk}} = \frac{c_k^r}{c^r_{max}} \leqslant 1$$

for all k. Thus $\underline{\lambda}' \epsilon \Lambda_s$ so Theorem 3 gives

$$R(D) \geqslant sD + \sum_j P_j \log \lambda_j' \quad , \quad \text{or}$$

$$R(D) \geqslant sD + \sum_j P_j \log \lambda_j^r - \log c^r_{max} = R_L^r(D)$$

which is the desired lower bound. Comparing the two bounds, we see that $I(Q^{r+1})$ differs from $R(d(Q^{r+1})) = R(D)$ by less than

$$R_U^r(D) - R_L^r(D) = \log c^r_{max} - \sum_k Q_k^r c_k^r \log c_k^r .$$

Since $1 \geqslant \lim_{r \to \infty} c_k^r$ with equality $\forall\, k \ni \lim_{r \to \infty} Q_k^r > 0$, we see that $\lim_{r \to \infty} R_U^r(D) - R_L^r(D) = 0$. The upper and lower bounds therefore tend to coincidence in the limit of large iteration number. If we need an estimate of R(D) with an error of ϵ or less, we need merely iterate on r until $\log c^r_{max} - \Sigma_k Q_k^r c_k^r \log c_k^r \leqslant \epsilon$. Note that both the iterations and the test to see if we are within ϵ of R(D) can be carried out without having to calculate either $I(Q^r)$ or $d(Q^r)$ at step r, let alone their gradients. This is the reason why the iterations proceed so rapidly in practice.

LECTURE 4.

Extension to Sources and Distortion Measures with Memory

We shall now indicate how to extend the theory developed above to cases in which the source and/or the distortion measure have memory. Let $P_n(x)$ denote the probability distribution governing the random source vector $\underline{X} = (X_1, \ldots, X_n)$, and let $\rho_n(\underline{x},\underline{y})$ denote the distortion incurred when the source vector $\underline{x}$ is reproduced as the vector y. Let $Q_n(\underline{y}/\underline{x})$ denote a hypothetical transition probability assignment, or "system", for transmission of successive blocks of length n. Then define

$$d(Q_n) = \sum_{\underline{x},\underline{y}} P_n(\underline{x}) Q_n(\underline{y}|\underline{x}) \rho_n(\underline{x},\underline{y})$$

$$I(Q_n) = n^{-1} \sum_{\underline{x},\underline{y}} P_n(\underline{x}) Q_n(\underline{y}|\underline{x}) \log \frac{Q_n(\underline{y}|\underline{x})}{Q_n(\underline{y})}$$

where

$$Q_n(\underline{y}) = \sum_{\underline{x}} P_n(\underline{x}) Q_n(\underline{y}|\underline{x}), \text{ and finally}$$

$$R_n(D) = \min_{Q_n : d(Q_n) \leqslant D} I(Q_n).$$

It is clear that $R_n(D)$ is the rate distortion function for a source that produces successive n-vectors independently according to $P_n(\underline{x})$ when the distortion in the reproduction of a sequence of such n-vectors is measured by the arithmetic average of ρ_n over the successive vectors that comprise the sequence. Although the actual source if stationary will produce successive n-vectors that are identically distributed according to $P_n(\underline{x})$, these vectors will not be independent. Hence, $R_n(D)$ will be an overestimate of the rate needed to achieve average distortion D because it does not reflect the fact that the statistical dependence between successive source letters can be exploited to further reduce the required information rate. However, one expects that this dependence will be useful only near the beginning and end of each block and hence may be ignored for large n. This tempted Shannon [2] to define

$$R(D) = \liminf_{n \to \infty} R_n(D)$$

Source coding theorems to the effect that the above prescription for calculating R(D) does indeed describe the absolute tradeoff between rate and distortion have been proven under increasingly general conditions by a variety of authors [2,4-9].

A sufficient but by no means necessary set of conditions is the following

(i) The source is strictly stationary

(ii) The source is ergodic

(iii) $\exists g < \infty$ and $\rho_g : A^g \times B^g \to [0,\infty]$ such that

$$\rho_n(\underline{x},\underline{y}) = \frac{1}{n-g+1} \sum_{t=1}^{n-g+1} \rho_g\left(x_t, x_{t+1}, \ldots, x_{t+g-1}, y_t, \ldots, y_{t+g-1}\right)$$

(This is called a distortion measure of span g and can be used to reflect context-dependencies when assigning distortions).

(iv) $$\exists\, \underline{y}^* \in B^g \quad \text{s.t.} \quad E_{\underline{X}} \rho_g(\underline{X}, \underline{y}^*) < \infty,$$

where $E_{\underline{X}}$ denotes expectation over a vector $\underline{X} = (X_1, \ldots, X_g)$ of g successive random source outputs.

Comments. Gray and Davisson [9] claim recently to have been able to remove the need for condition (ii). Condition (iv) is automatically satisfied to finite-alphabet sources; it is needed only when the theory is extended to the important case of sources with continuous, possibly unbounded, source alphabets.

Under conditions (i) and (iii) the $R_n(D)$ curves will be monotonic nonincreasing for $n \geq g$. They have the physical significance that no system that operates independently on successive n-vectors from the source can perform below $R_n(D)$. However, the corresponding positive source coding theorem that systems can be found that operate arbitrarily close to $R_n(D)$ is true only in the limit $n \to \infty$.

We now give some explicit examples of rate distortion functions.

Example 1. Binary Memoryless Source and Error Frequence Criterion [Shannon, 1948, 1959; Goblick, 1962]

$$A = B = \{0,1\} \ , \ \rho_{jk} = 1 - \delta_{jk} = \begin{cases} 0 \text{ if } j = k \\ 1 \text{ if } j \neq k. \end{cases}$$

Assume that zeros are produced with probability $1-p \geq 1/2$ and ones with probability $p \leq 1/2$.

A simple computation shows that

$$R(D) = \begin{cases} H_b(p) - H_b(D), & 0 \leq D \leq D_{max} = p \\ 0 & , D \geq p \end{cases}$$

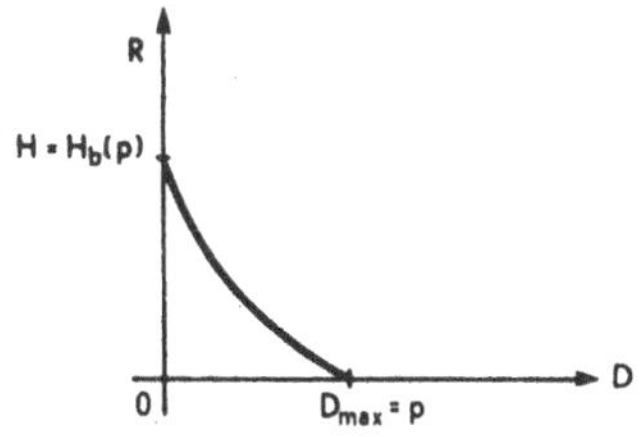

where $H_b(.)$ is the binary entropy function,

$$H_b(p) = -p \log p - (1-p) \log(1-p)$$

In the equiprobable case $p=1/2$, we get

$$R(D) = 1 + D \log_2 D + (1-D) \log_2 (1-D) \quad \text{bits/letter}$$

This formula equals the Gilbert bound which is a lower bound on the exponential rate of growth of the maximum number of vectors that can be packed into binary n-space such that no two of them disagree in fewer than nD places. Rate distortion theory yields a different interpretation of this curve in terms of covering theory. Namely, $R(D) = 1 + D \log_2 D + (1-D) \log_2 (1-D)$ is the exponential rate of growth of the minimum number of vectors such that every point in binary n space differs from at least one of these vectors in fewer than nD places. Note that in the covering problem the result is exact, whereas in the corresponding packing problem the tightest upper bounds known (Elias[10], Levenstein[11]) are strictly greater than the Gilbert bound*. In this sense at least covering problems are simpler than packing problems.

Example 2. Gaussian Source and Mean Squared Error (MSE) [Shannon, 1948, and 1959]

*It is widely believed that the Hilbert bound is tight in the packing problem, too, but no proof has been found despite more than 20 years of attempts.

$A = B = \mathcal{R}$, the real line $\rho(x,y) = (x-y)^2$.

The source letters are governed by the Gaussian probability density

$$p(x) = \frac{e^{-\frac{(x-\mu)^2}{2\sigma^2}}}{\sqrt{2\pi\sigma^2}}, \quad x \in \mathcal{R}$$

The R(D) curve given by Shannon [1,12] is

$$R(D) = \frac{1}{2}\log(\sigma^2/D) \quad , \; 0 \leqslant D \leqslant D_{max} = \sigma^2$$

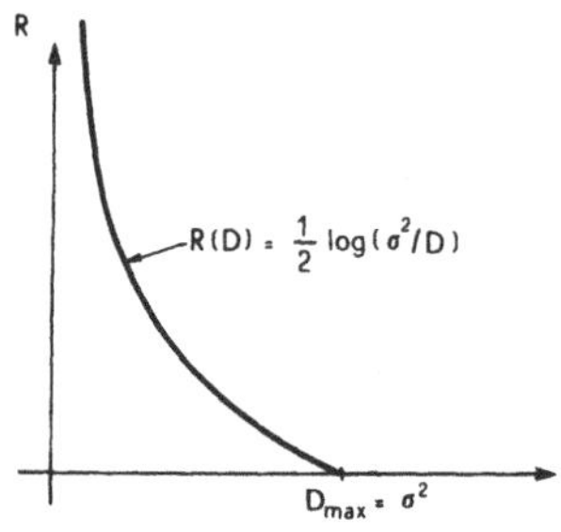

Example 3. Stationary Gaussian Random Sequence and MSE [Kolmogorov, 1956]

$$A = B = \mathcal{R}$$

$$\rho(x,y) = (x-y)^2$$

$$E[X_i X_{i+k}] = \varphi_k \quad , \quad EX_i = 0,$$

The answer is most easily expressed in terms of the discrete-time spectral density

$$\Phi(\omega) = \sum_{k=-\infty}^{\infty} \varphi_k e^{-ik\omega} \quad , \quad i^2 = -1$$

The R and D coordinates are then given parametrically in terms of $\theta \in [0, \sup_w \Phi(\omega)]$ as follows :

$$D_\theta = \frac{1}{2\pi}\int_{-\pi}^{\pi} \min[\theta, \Phi(\omega)]\, d\omega$$

$$R(D_\theta) = \frac{1}{4\pi}\int_{-\pi}^{\pi} \max[0, \log \Phi(\omega)/\theta]\, d\omega$$

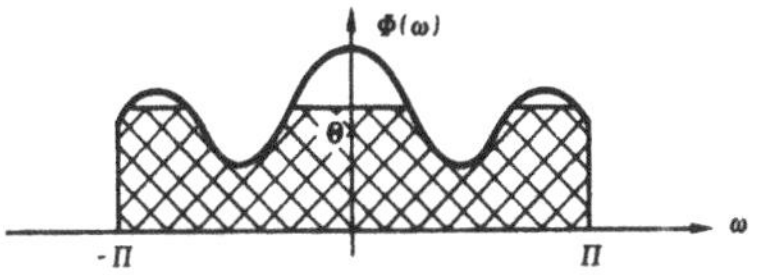

The cross-hatched region in the accompanying sketch is the area under the so-called "error spectrum", $\min[\theta, \Phi(\omega)]$, associated with the parameter θ. The optimum system for rate $R(D_\theta)$ will yield a reproduction sequence $\{Y_i\}$ which is Gaussian and stationarily related to $\{X_i\}$ with the error sequence $\{X_i - Y_i\}$ having time-discrete spectral density/min $[\theta, \Phi(\omega)]$, $|\omega| \leq \pi$.

Example 4. Stationary Gaussian Random Process and MSE [Kolmogorov, 1956]

Let

$$\underline{x} = \{x(t), 0 \leq t \leq T\}, \quad \underline{y} = \{y(t), 0 \leq t \leq T\}$$

and

$$\rho_T(x,y) = \frac{1}{T}\int_0^T [x(t) - y(t)]^2 dt.$$

The formulas for D_θ and $R(D_\theta)$ from the time-discrete case of Example 3 continue to apply except that the limits on the integrals become $\pm\infty$ instead of $\pm\pi$ and the spectral density $\Phi(\omega)$ is defined by

$$\Phi(\omega) = \int_{-\infty}^{\infty} \varphi(\tau) e^{-j\omega\tau} d\tau$$

where

$$\varphi(\tau) = E[X(t)X(t+\tau)].$$

In the special case of an ideal bandlimited process

$$\Phi(\omega) = \begin{cases} \Phi_0, & |\omega| \leq 2\pi W \\ 0, & |\omega| > 2\pi W \end{cases}$$

the results specialize to $D_\theta = 2W\theta$ and $R(D_\theta) = W \log(\Phi_0/\theta)$. Eliminating θ yields the explicit result

$$R(D) = W \log\left(\frac{2W\Phi_0}{D}\right)$$

Now the instantaneous signal power is

$$S = \frac{1}{2\pi}\int_{-\infty}^{\infty}\Phi(\omega)\,d\omega = \frac{1}{2\pi}\int_{-2\pi W}^{2\pi W}\Phi_0\,d\omega = 2W\Phi_0 ,$$

and the mean squared error D in the reconstruction of the signal can be considered as an effective additive noise power N, the above result often is written as

$$R(D) = W \log\left(\frac{S}{N}\right),$$

which is the form originally given by Shannon [1].

LECTURE 5.

Algebraic Source Encoding

We shall now prove the source coding theorem for the special case of the binary equiprobable memoryless source and error frequency fidelity criterion (Example 1 with $p = 1/2$). Moreover, the proof will show that a sequence of linear codes of increasing blocklength n can be found whose (D,R) performances converge to any specified point on the rate distortion function, $R(D) = 1 - H_b(D)$ bits/letter. The fact that the codes in question are linear is very important from the practical standpoint because the associated structure considerably simplifies the encoding procedure.

Let $\underline{x} = (x_1, \dots, x_n) \in \{0,1\}^n$ and $\underline{y} = \in \{0,1\}^n$ denote a typical source vector and reproduction vector, respectively. Define

$$S_\ell(\underline{y}) = \{\underline{x} : d_H(\underline{x},\underline{y}) \leqslant \ell\}$$

where d_H is the Hamming distance function.

Given any set $\underline{y}_1, \underline{y}_2, \dots, \underline{y}_j$ of not necessarily t linearly independent reproduction vectors, let

$$B_j = \{\underline{y}_1, \underline{y}_2, \dots, \underline{y}_{2^j}\}$$

denote the $[n, j]$ linear code with generators $\underline{y}_1, \dots, \underline{y}_j$ (If the generators are not linearly independent, then not all 2^j of the $\underline{y}_i \in B_j$ are distinct). For completeness, let $B_0 = \{\underline{0}\}$. Define

$$F_j = \bigcup_{\underline{y} \in B_j} S_\ell(\underline{y}),$$

and let $N_j = \|F_j\|$ denote the cardinality of F_j. It should be clear that N_j is the number of source vectors $\underline{x}$ that can be encoded by at least one $\underline{y} \in B_j$ with error frequency ℓ/n or less. Accordingly, the probability Q_j that a random vector $\underline{X}$ produced by the source cannot be encoded by B_j with average distortion ℓ/n or less is

$$Q_j = 1 - 2^{-n} N_j$$

because all 2^n possible values of $\underline{X}$ are equally likely.

Now consider the addition of another generator $\underline{y}_{j+1}$ resulting in a code B_{j+1}. Then

$$F_{j+1} = F_j \cup F_j^*$$

where

$$F_j^* = \bigcup_{\underline{y} \in B_j} S_\ell(\underline{y} + \underline{y}_{j+1}) = \{\underline{v} + \underline{y}_{j+1} : \underline{v} \in F_j\}$$

The set F_j^* clearly is geometrically isomorphic to F_j and therefore contains N_j elements, too. It follows that

$$N_{j+1} = 2N_j - \|F_j \cap F_j^*\|$$

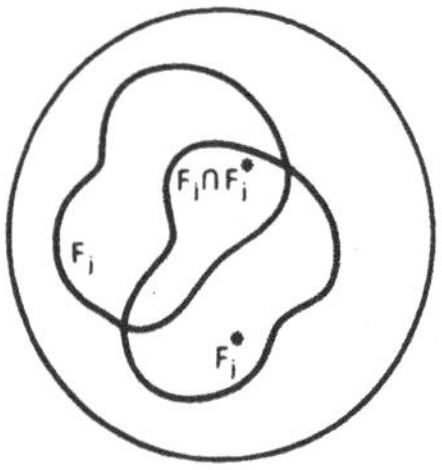

A good choice of $\underline{y}_{j+1}$ is one that makes $\|F_j \cap F_j^*\|$ small. We proceed to derive an upper bound that we are assured will exceed $\|F_j \cap F_j^*\|$ for some choice of $\underline{y}_{j+1}$. This is done by averaging $\|F_j \cap F_j^*\|$ over all 2^n possible choices of $\underline{y}_{j+1}$ and then concluding that there must be at least one $\underline{y}_{j+1}$ such that $\|F_j \cap F_j^*\|$ does not exceed this average. The average is calculated by observing that, for fixed $\underline{v} \in F_j$, the vector $\underline{v} + \underline{y}_{j+1} \in F_j^*$ also belongs to F_j iff $\underline{y}_{j+1} = \underline{v} + \underline{u}$ for some $u \in F_j$. Hence, there are exactly N_j choices of $\underline{y}_{j+1}$ such that $\underline{v} + \underline{y}_{j+1} \in F_j \cap F_j^*$. Now letting $\underline{v}$ vary over the N_j points of F_j shows that there are a total of $N_j \cdot N_j = N_j^2$ pairs $(\underline{v}, \underline{y}_{j+1})$, $\underline{v} \in F_j$, such that $\underline{v} + \underline{y}_{j+1} \in F_j \cap F_j^*$. It follows that the average value of $\|F_j \cap F_j^*\|$ is $2^{-n} N_j^2$. Therefore, there exists at least one way to choose $\underline{y}_{j+1}$ such that

$$N_{j+1} \geqslant 2N_j - 2^{-n} N_j^2$$

This implies that

$$Q_{j+1} = 1 - 2^{-n} N_{j+1} \leq 1 - 2 \cdot 2^{-n} N_j + (2^{-n} N_j)^2$$

$$Q_{j+1} \leq (1 - 2^{-n} N_j)^2 = Q_j^2$$

It follows by recursion that

$$Q_k \leq Q_o^{2^k} = (1 - 2^{-n} N_o)^{2^k}$$

Since

$$N_o = \| S_\ell(\underline{0}) \| = \sum_{i=0}^{\ell} \binom{n}{i} \geq \binom{n}{\ell} ,$$

$$\begin{aligned} Q_k &\leq \left[1 - 2^{-n}\binom{n}{\ell}\right]^{2^k} \\ &= \exp\left\{2^k \log\left[1 - 2^{-n}\binom{n}{\ell}\right]\right\} \\ &\leq \exp\left[-2^k\, 2^{-n}\binom{n}{\ell}\right] \end{aligned}$$

where we have used the fundamental inequality in the last step. Now let $n \to \infty$ and $k \to \infty$ in such a way that the code rate $k/n \to R$, and let $\ell \to \infty$ such that $\ell/n \to D$. It then follows that the probability Q_k that the source produces a word that cannot be encoded with distortion D or less will tend to zero provided

$$\lim_{\substack{n \to \infty \\ k/n \to R \\ \ell/n \to D}} 2^k\, 2^{-n}\binom{n}{\ell} = \infty$$

Since by Stirling's approximation we know that

$$\binom{n}{nD} \sim 2^{\,nH_b(D) \pm O(n^{\frac{1}{2}} \log n)} ,$$

we conclude that $Q_k \to 0$ provided $nR - n + nH_b(D) \to \infty$,i.e., provided

$$R > 1 - H_b(D) = R(D) .$$

Hence, we have established the following theorem.

Theorem 4. [Goblick, 1962]

There exist D–admissible linear codes of rate R for the binary equiprobable memoryless source and error frequency criterion for any $R > R(D) = 1 - H_b(D)$ bits/letter.

The encoding, or compression, of binary data by means of a linear code proceeds in exact analogy to the procedure for decoding the word received at the channel output in the channel coding application. Specifically, when the source produces $\underline{x}$, one computes the syndrome

$$\underline{s} = H\underline{x}^T$$

and then searches for a minimum weight solution $\underline{z}$ of the equation

$$\underline{s} = H\underline{z}^T .$$

Such a $\underline{z}$ is called the leader of the coset $C(\underline{s}) = \{\underline{v} : H\underline{v}^T = \underline{s}\}$. Once $\underline{z}$ has been found, which is the hardest part of the procedure, one then encodes (approximates) $\underline{x}$ by $\underline{y} = \underline{x} + \underline{z}$. Said $\underline{y}$ is a code word since $H\underline{y}^T = H\underline{x}^T + H\underline{z}^T = \underline{s} + \underline{s} = \underline{0}$. Hence, $\underline{y}$ is expressible as a linear combination (mod. 2) of the k generators. This means that a string of k binary digits suffices for specification of $\underline{y}$. In this way the n source digits are compressed to only k digits that need to be transmitted. The resulting error frequency is $n^{-1}wt(\underline{x}-\underline{y}) = n^{-1}wt(\underline{z})$. Accordingly, the expected error frequency D is the average weight of the coset leaders

$$D = n^{-1} 2^{-(n-k)} \sum_{i=1}^{2^{n-k}} w_i$$

where w_i is the weight of the leader $\underline{z}_i$ of the ith coset, $1 \leq i \leq 2^{n-k}$. It follows that for the source encoding application the crucial parameter of an algebraic code is the average weight of its coset leaders rather than the minimum distance between any pair of codewords.

LECTURE 6

Tree Codes for Sources

There are two major difficulties with algebraic source encoding. The first one is that most sources do not naturally produce outputs in GF(q) for some prime power q. Of course, the source outputs can be losslessly encoded into a string of elements from GF(q), but then it is unlikely that minimization of Hamming or Lee distance will correspond to maximization of fidelity. The second difficulty is that, even if $A = GF(q)$ and the Hamming or Lee metric is appropriate, the source produces output vectors that are distributed over A^n in a manner that does not concentrate probability in the immediate vicinity of the code words. This differs markedly from the situation that prevails in channel decoding where the probability distribution on the space of channel output vectors is concentrated in peaks centered at the code words (provided the code rate is not extremely close to the channel capacity). As a result it suffices

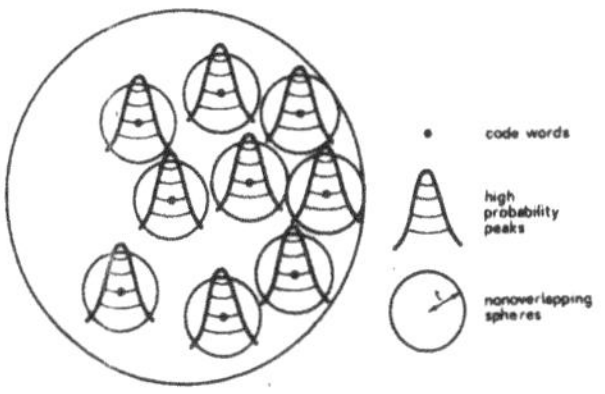

Figure 4. Sketch of Probability Distribution Over the Space of Channel Output Words

in most instances to limit decoding to the nonoverlapping spheres of radius $t \approx d/2$ centered about the codewords. The majority of algebraic decoding procedures that have been devised to date simply abort whenever the received word does not lie inside one of the spheres of radius t centered at the code words. Such decoding procedures are essentially useless for source encoding because the source word density is just as great between these spheres as it is inside them. In fact, if one insists that the limiting rate of a sequence of binary codes be bounded away from 0 and 1 as $n \to \infty$, then a vanishingly small fraction of the space will lie within the nonoverlapping t-spheres.

It follows from the above discussion that a good algebraic source encoding algorithm must be complete in the sense that it finds the closest (or at least a close) code word for every possible received word. At present complete decoding algorithms are known only for the Hamming codes [Hamming, 1950], $t = 2$ BCH codes [Berlekamp, 1968], certain $t = 3$ BCH codes [Berger and Van der Horst, 1973], and first-order Reed-Muller codes [Posner, 1968]. Unfortunately, the asymptotic rate is 1 for these Hamming and BCH codes, and 0 for these Reed-Muller codes, so no long, good, decodable algebraic source codes of nontrivial rate are known at present.

Another way to introduce structure into a source code that overcomes most of the shortcomings of the algebraic approach is to employ tree codes. The concept of tree encoding of sources is most readily introduced by means of an example. The tree code depicted in Figure 5 provides a means for encoding the binary source of Example 1 of Lecture 4.

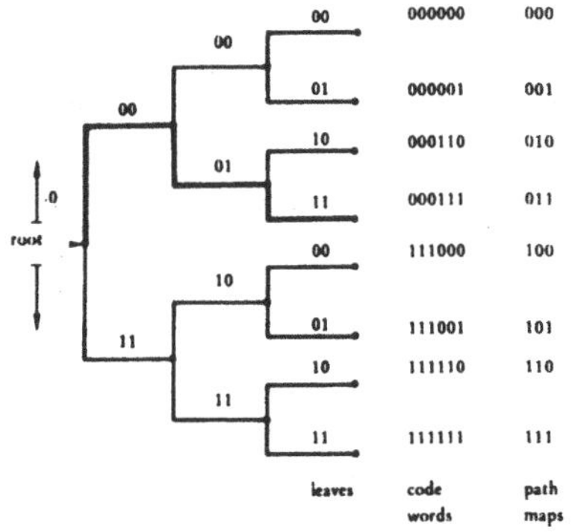

Figure 5. A Binary Tree Code

The code consists of the $2^3 = 8$ different words of length $n = 6$ that can be formed by concatenating the three pairs of binary digits encountered along a path from the root to a leaf. The code word corresponding to each such path is indicated in Figure 5 directly to the right of the leaf at which the path terminates. Since there are $2^6 = 64$ different words of length 6 that might be produced by the source, there usually will not be a code word that matches the source word exactly. Accordingly, we approximate the source word $\underline{x}$ by whatever $\underline{y}$ in the code minimizes $\rho_6(\underline{x},\underline{y})$. For example, if $\underline{x} = 010110$, then $\underline{y} = 000110$ is closest in the sense of the Hamming metric. When traversing the path from the root to the leaf $\underline{y} = 000110$, we branch first up, then down, and then up at the successive nodes encountered. Hence, this path is specified by the binary path map sequence 010, where 0 represents "up" and 1 represents "down". In this way we have compressed a source sequence of length 6 into a path map of length 3. Despite the fact that the data rate has been compressed by a factor of two, most of the original source digits can be recovered correctly. The reader may wish to verify that in the equiprobable case $p = 1/2$, the average fraction of the digits that are reproduced incorrectly is

3/16 = 0.1875. The best that could be done in this instance by any code of rate R=1/2 of any blocklength is D(R=1/2) = 0.110.

It should be clear that tree codes can be designed with any desired rate. If there are b branches per node and ℓ letters per branch, then the rate is

$$R = \ell^{-1} \log d$$

Also, the letters on the branches can be chosen from any reproducing alphabet whatsoever including a continuous alphabet, so tree coding is not restricted to GF(q).

Tree encoding of sources was first proposed by Goblick (1962). Jelinek (1969) proved that tree codes can be found that perform arbitrarily close to the R(D) curve for any memoryless source and fidelity criterion; this result has been extended by Berger (1971) to a limited class of sources with memory. In order for tree coding to become practical, however, an efficient search algorithm must be devised for finding a good path through the tree. (Note that, unlike in sequential decoding for channels, one need not necessarily find the best path through the tree; a good path will suffice). This problem has been attacked with some degree of success by Anderson and Jelinek (1971, 1973), by Gallager (1973), by Viterbi and Omura (1973), and by Berger, Dick and Jelinek (1973).

In conclusion, it should be mentioned that delta modulation and more general differential PCM schemes are special examples of tree encoding procedures. However, even the adaptive versions of such schemes are necessarily sub-optimal because they make their branching decisions instantaneously on the basis solely of past and present source outputs. Performance could be improved by introducing some coding delay in order to take future source outputs into consideration, too.

LECTURE 7

Theory vs Practice and Some Open Problems

In the final lecture of this overview of rate distortion theory, I shall begin by attempting to convey some feeling for the current status of the comparison of theory and practice in data compression. I shall couch the discussion in terms of the i.i.d. Gaussian source and MSE criterion of Example 2 of Lecture 4 because this example has been treated the most thoroughly in the literature. However, the overall flavor of my comments applies to more general sources and distortion measures, too.

Recall that the rate distortion function for the situation in question is

$$R(D) = \frac{1}{2} \log (\sigma^2 / D)$$

When this is plotted with a logarithmic D-axis, it appears as a straight line with negative slope as sketched in Figure 6. Parallel to R(D)

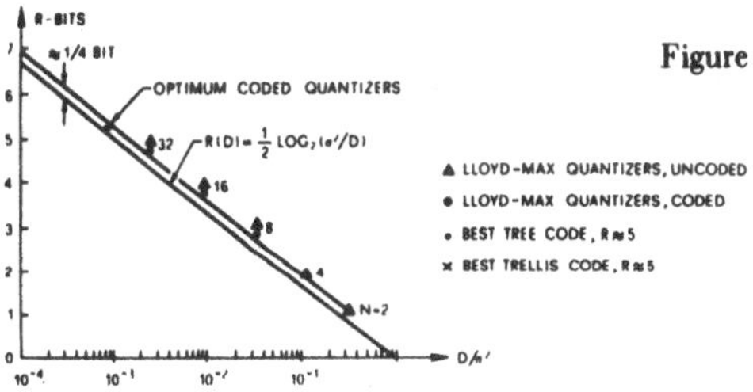

Figure 6. Performances for Gauss-MSE Problem

but approximately 1/4bit higher lies the performance curve of the best entropy-coded quantizers. The small separation indicates that there is very little to be gained by more sophisticated encoding techniques. This is not especially surprising given the memoryless nature of both the source and the fidelity criterion. It must be emphasized, however, that entropy coding necessitates the use of a buffer to implement the conversion to variable-length codewords. Moreover, since the optimum quantizer has nearly uniformly spaced levels, some of these levels become many times more probable than others, which leads to difficult buffering problems. Furthermore, when the buffer overflows it is usually because of an inordinately high local density of large-magnitude source outputs. This means that the per-letter MSE incurred when buffer overflows occur tends to be even bigger than σ^2.

As a result, the performance of coded quantizers with buffer overflow properly taken into account may be considerably poorer than that shown in Figure 6, especially at high rates.

The buffering problem can be circumvented by not applying entropy coding to the quantizer outputs. However, the performance curves of uncoded quantizer diverge from R(D) at high R, as indicated by the locus of uncoded Lloyd-Max quantizers in Figure 6.

Another scheme studied by Berger, Jelinek and Wolf (1972) uses the permutation codes of Slepian (1965) in reverse for compression of source data. The performance curve of optimum permutation codes of fixed blocklength and varying rate essentially coincides with the optimum coded quantizer curve for low rates but diverges from it at a rate that increases with blocklength. Permutation codes offer the advantage of synchronous operation, but they are characterized by long coding delays and the need to partially order the components of the source vector. Berger (1972) has shown that optimum quantizers and optimum permutation codes perform identically in the respective limits of perfect entropy coding and of infinite blocklength. Both are strictly bounded away from R(D).

An extensive study of tree coding techniques for the Gauss-MSE problem was undertaken by Berger, Dick and Jelinek (1973). They studied source encoding adaptations of both the Jelinek-Zigangirov stack algorithm for sequential decoding of channel tree codes and the Viterbi algorithm for trellis codes. The best performances obtained, determined by extensive simulation, were strictly better than that of the best coded quantizer as indicated by the points marked in Figure 6. The best stack algorithm run had $D = 1.243D(R)$ and the Viterbi algorithm achieved $D = 1.308\ D(R)$, whereas coded quantizers achieve at best $D = 1.415\ D(R)$. However, it was necessary to search 512 nodes per datum in the Viterbi runs and an average of 727 nodes per datum in the best of the stack runs.
Hence, real time tree encoding of practical analog sources at high rates is not instrumentable at present.

We close with a discussion of several open problems and research areas.

A. Algebraic Source Encoding

1. Derive bounds on the average weights of the coset leaders of families of linear codes.
2. Are long BCH, Justesen, and/or Goppa source codes good?
3. Find complete decoding algorithms for families of codes with nondegenerate

asymptotic rates.

4. Prove that the ensemble performance of codes with generators chosen independently at random approaches R(D) as $n \to \infty$.
5. Extend the theory satisfactorily to nonequiprobable sources.

B. Tree Coding

1. Show that there are good convolutional tree codes for sources. (For continuous amplitude sources the tapped shift register is replaced by a feed-forward digital fitter.
2. Find better algorithms for finding satisfactory paths through the tree (or trellis).

C. Information-Singularity [Berger (1973)]

Characterize the class of all sources whose MSE rate distortion functions vanish $\forall D > 0$. This class is surprisingly broad, and its study promises to provide insight into the fundamental structure of information production mechanisms.

D. Biochemical Data Compression

The equations in chemical thermodynamics that describe the approach to multiphase chemical equilibrium are mathematically analogous to those which must be solved in order to calculate a point on an R(D) curve. It has been postulated [Berger (1971)] that this is not purely coincidental; indeed, the interaction of a living system with its environment can be modeled by multiphase chemical equilibrium. By "solving" this multiphase chemical equilibrium problem, the system efficiently extracts those aspects of the environmental data that it wishes to record accurately and either rejects or only coarsely encodes the remainder.

The provocative mathematical analogy with rate distortion theory arises as follows.

If n_j molecules of substance j, $1 \leq j \leq M$, are injected into a system that possesses N thermodynamically homogeneous phases, then the number n_{jk} of molecules of substance j that reside in phase k at equilibrium is found by minimizing the Gibbs free energy functional which has the form

$$F = \sum_{j,k} n_{jk} \left[\log\left(\frac{n_{jk}}{n_k}\right) + C_{jk} \right],$$

where $n_k = \sum_j n_{jk}$ and the C_{jk}, are so-called "free energy constants" that can be experimentally measured. The minimization naturally is subject to the mass balance conditions $\sum_k n_{jk} = n_j$ and the constraints $n_{jk} \geqslant 0$. Letting $n = \sum_j n_j$ and making the obvious associations

$$n_j \sim nP_j$$

$$n_{jk} \sim nP_j\, Q_{k/j}$$

$$n_k \sim nQ_k$$

$$C_{jk} \sim -s\rho_{jk}$$

one finds that F is of the form $F = I(Q) - sd(Q)$, which we know from earlier work to be the quantity that one must minimize to find the point on R(D) at which the slope is s.

Investigation of the realm of applicability of rate distortion theory to environmental encoding by biochemical systems along the lines of the above discussion of multiphase chemical equilibrium appears to be a very worthwhile area for future research. It may well turn out that principal usefulness of rate distortion theory will prove to be in applications to biology rather than to communication theory.

REFERENCES

[1] SHANNON, C.E., (1948). "A Mathematical Theory of Communication", BSTJ, 27, 379-423, 623-656.

[2] SHANNON, C.E., (1959) "Coding Theorems for a Discrete Source with a Fidelity Criterion", IRE Nat'l. Conv. Rec., Part 4, 142-163.

[3] BLAHUT, R.E., (1972) "Computation of Channel Capacity and Rate-distortion Functions", Trans. IEEE, IT-18, 460-473.

[4] PINKSTER, M.S., (1963) "Sources of Messages", Problemy Peredecii Informatsii. 14, 5-20.

[5] GALLAGER, R.G., (1968) "Information Theory and Reliable Communication", Wiley, New York.

[6] BERGER, T., (1968) "Rate Distortion Theory for Sources with Abstract Alphabets and Memory", Information and Control, 13, 254-273.

[7] GOBLICK, T.J., Jr. (1969) "A Coding Theorem for Time-Discrete Analog Data Sources", Trans. IEEE, IT-15, 401-407.

[8] BERGER, T., (1971) "Rate Distortion Theory. A Mathematical Basis for Data Compression", Prentice-Hall, Englewood Cliffs, N.Y.

[9] GRAY, R.M., and L.D. DAVISSON (1973) "Source Coding Without Ergodicity", Presented at 1973 IEEE Intern. Symp. on Inform. Theory, Ashkelon, Israel.

[10] GOBLICK, T.J., Jr. (1962) "Coding for a Discrete Information Source with a Distortion Measure", Ph.D.Dissertation, Elec. Eng. Dept. M.I.T. Cambridge, Mass.

[11] KOLMOGOROV, A.N., (1956) "On the Shannon Theory of Information

Transmission in the Case of Continuous Signals", Trans. IEEE, IT-2, 102-108.

[12] HAMMING, R.W., (1950) "Error Detecting and Error Correcting Codes", BSTJ, 29, 147-160.

[13] BERLEKAMP, E.R., (1968) "Algebraic Coding Theory", McGraw-Hill, N.Y.

[14] BERGER, T., and J.A. VAN DER HORST (1973) "BCH Source Codes", Submitted to IEEE Trans. on Information Theory.

[15] POSNER, E.C., (1968) In Man H.B."Error Correcting Codes", Wiley, N.Y. Chapter 2.

[16] JELINEK, F., (1969) "Tree Encoding of Memoryless Time-Discrete Sources with a Fidelity Criterion", Trans. IEEE, IT-15, 584-590.

[17] JELINEK, F., and J.B. ANDERSON (1971) "Instrumentable Tree Encoding and Information Sources", Trans. IEEE, IT-17, 118-119.

[18] ANDERSON, J.B., and F. JELINEK (1973) "A Two-Cycle Algorithm for Source Coding with a Fidelity Criterion", Trans. IEEE, IT-19, 77-92.

[19] GALLAGER, R.G., (1973) "Tree Encoding for Symmetric Sources with a Distortion Measure", Presented at 1973 IEEE Int'l. Symp. on Information Theory, Ashkelon, Israel.

[20] VITERBI, A.J., and J.K. OMURA (1974) "Trellis Encoding of Memoryless Discrete-Time Sources with a Fidelity Criterion", Trans. IEEE, IT-20, 325-332.

[21] BERGER, T., R.J. DICK and F. JELINEK (1974) "Tree Encoding of Gaussian Sources", Trans. IEEE, IT-20, 332-336.

[22] BERGER, T., F. JELINEK and J.K. WOLF (1972) "Permutation Codes for Sources", Trans. IEEE, IT-18, 160-169.

[23] SLEPIAN, D., (1965) "Permutation Modulation", Proc. IEEE, 53, 228-236.

[24] BERGER, T., (1972) "Optimum Quantizers and Permutation Codes", Trans. IEEE, IT-18, 759-765.

[25] BERGER, T., (1973) "Information - Singular Random Processes", Presented at Third International Symposium on Information Theory, Tallinn, Estonia, USSR.

UNIVERSAL SOURCE CODING

LEE D. DAVISSON
Department of Electrical Engineering
University of Southern California, Berkeley

PREFACE

I am grateful to Professor Giuseppe Longo for inviting me to participate in this workshop and for the opportunity to present the series of lectures represented by the following notes.

Lee D. Davisson

I. Introduction

A. Summary

The basic purpose of data compression is to massage a data stream to reduce the average bit rate required for transmission or storage by removing unwanted redundancy and/or unnecessary precision. A mathematical formulation of data compression providing figures of merit and bounds on optimal performance was developed by Shannon [1,2] both for the case where a perfect compressed reproduction is required and for the case where a certain specified average distortion is allowable. Unfortunately, however, Shannon's probabilistic approach requires advance precise knowledge of the statistical description of the process to be compressed - a demand rarely met in practice. The coding theorems only apply, or are meaningful, when the source is stationary and ergodic.

We here present a tutorial description of numerous recent approaches and results generalizing the Shannon approach to unknown statistical environments. Simple examples and empirical results are given to illustrate the essential ideas.

B. Source Modelling

Sources with unknown statistical descriptions or with incomplete or inaccurate statistical descriptions can be modelled as a class of sources from which nature chooses a particular source and reveals only its outputs and not the source chosen. The size and content of the class are determined by our knowledge or lack thereof about the possible source probabilities. Typical classes might be the class of all stationary sources with a given alphabet, the class of all Bernoulli processes (sequences of independent, identically distributed binary random variables, i.e., coin flipping with all possible biases), the class of all Gaussian random processes with bounded covariances and means, etc.

The source chosen by Nature can be modelled as a random variable, i.e., a random choice described by a prior probability distribution, or it can be modelled as a fixed but unknown source, i.e., we have no such prior.

To model such a class, assume that for each value of an index $\theta \in \Lambda$ we have a discrete time source $\{X_n ; n = \ldots,-1,0,1,\ldots\}$ with some alphabet A of possible outputs and a statistical description μ_θ, specifically, μ_θ is a probability measure on a sample space of all possible doubly infinite sequences drawn from A (and an appropriate σ - field of subsets called events). Thus μ_θ implies the probability distributions on all random vectors composed of a finite number of samples of the process, e.g., μ_θ implies for any integer N the distributions μ_θ^N describing the random vector $X^N \triangleq (X_1, \ldots, X_N)$. As noted above, the source index may (or may not) itself be considered as a random variable Ⓗ taking values in the parameter space Λ as described by some prior probability distribution $W(\theta)$. The source described by μ_θ will often be referred to simply as θ. Similarly, the class will often be abbreviated to Λ.

We shall usually assume that the individual sources θ are stationary, i.e., the statistical description μ_θ is invariant to shifts of the time origin. We shall sometimes require also that the individual sources be ergodic, that is, with μ_θ -probability-one all sample functions produced by the source are representative of the source in that all sample moments converge to appropriate expectations and all relative frequencies of events converge to the appropriate probabilities. This should not be considered as a limitation on the theory since in practice, most real sources can be considered to have at least local (i.e., over each output block presented to an encoder) stationary and ergodic properties.

From the ergodic decomposition of a stationary time series [3,4,5], any stationary nonergodic source can be viewed as a class of ergodic sources with a prior. Hence, stationary nonergodic sources are included in our model and the subsources in a class of stationary sources can be considered ergodic without loss of generality, i.e., a class of stationary sources can be decomposed into a "finer" class of ergodic sources.

For example, consider a Bernoulli source, i.e., a binary source in which the probability θ of a "one" chosen by "nature" randomly according to the uniform probability law on [0,1] and then fixed for all time. The user is not told θ, however. Subsequently the source produces independent-letter outputs with the chosen, but unknown, probability. The probability, given θ, that any message block of length N contains n ones in any given pattern is then

$$\theta^n (1-\theta)^{N-n}$$

Given θ the source is stationary and ergodic. Otherwise the source is stationary only and the probability of any given message containing n ones in N outputs is simply

$$\int_0^1 \theta^n (1-\theta)^{N-n} \, d\theta = \frac{1}{N+1} \binom{N}{n}^{-1} .$$

The relative frequency of ones for this source converges to Θ, a random variable. It is seen that the stationary source can be decomposed by working backwards into an ergodic class of subsources indexed by θ.

The object of data compression is to process the observed source messages to reduce the bit rate required for transmission. If the compressed reproduction is required to be perfect (noiseless source coding), then compression can only be achieved through the removal of unnecessary redundancy. If the compressed reproduction need not be perfect (as is usually the case with continuous alphabets), but need only satisfy some average fidelity constraint, then compression can also be achieved via removal of unnecessary precision (as in quantization).

We shall here consider only block processors, i.e., compressors that operate on individual consecutive source blocks or vectors $X_i^N = (X_{iN}, X_{iN+1}, \ldots, X_{iN+N-1})$, $i = 0,1,\ldots$, independently of previous or future blocks. The index i will be suppressed subsequently. The block coder maps X^N into a reproduction $\hat{x}(X^N)$. The block coding restriction eliminates such methods as run–length encoding, but is made for analytical simplicity and the fact that block encoders provide a large and useful class.

The classical Shannon theory [1,2] provides figures of merit and bounds on optimal performance for block-encoders (hereafter called simply encoders) $\hat{x}(X^N)$ when the source is stationary and ergodic and the source probabilities are known precisely. Universal coding is the extension of these ideas to the more general situation of a class of sources, wherein encoders must be designed without precise knowledge of the actual statistics of the source to be observed, or equivalently, where the source is nonergodic. The encoder is called "universal" if the performance of the code designed without knowledge of the unknown "true" source converges in the limit of long blocklength N to the optimal performance possible if one knew the true source. Different types of universality are defined to correspond to different notions of convergence.

In this tutorial presentation of recent approaches and results on noiseless universal encoding and universal coding subject to a rate or an average fidelity constraint, we attempt a unified development with a minimum of uniformative mathematical detail and a maximum of intuition. As the mere existence of universal codes is suprising, the first cases considered are nearly trivial in order to make these types of results believable and to emphasize the fundamental ideas in the simplest possible context.

The mathematical detail, the proofs of the general theorem, and complete historical references may be found in [4,10].

II. Variable-Rate Noiseless Source Codes

We first consider uniquely decodeable block-to-variable length source codes. As we here require perfect reproduction, the alphabet A is assumed discrete. Given a blocklength N, a code C_N is a codebook or collection of codewords or vectors of varying blocklength and an encoding rule $\hat{x}(X^N)$ that assigns to each possible source N-tuple a unique codeword. $\mathcal{C}(N)$ is the class of all uniquely decodeable codes C_N. In this situation compression is achieved by minimizing the average length of the codewords and hence minimizing the average bit rate required to perfectly communicate the source. Thus the principal property of interest of a code C_N is the resulting average length of codewords when applying the code to a particular source. For a given C_N, define the normalized length function $\ell(x^N | C_N)$ as N^{-1} times the codeword length in bits of $\hat{x}(x^N)$, the codeword resulting when C_N is used to encode the source block x^N. Given a particular source described by μ_θ, define the average normalized length resulting from using the code C_N on this source by

$$\ell_\theta(C_N) = E_\theta[\ell(x^N | C_N)]$$

where E_θ denotes expectation over μ_θ, i.e., since the alphabet is discrete

$$E_\theta[\ell(x^N | C_N)] = \sum_{x^N} \ell(x^N | C_N)\mu_\theta^N(x^N)$$

where μ_θ^N is taken as the probability mass function of N-tuples.

The optimal code in $\mathcal{C}(N)$ is the one that minimizes the average normalized length. Define

$$\lambda_\theta(N) = \inf_{C_N \in \mathcal{C}(N)} \ell_\theta(C_N)$$

as the minimal attainable average normalized length using block-length N-to variable-length codes on θ. Define

$$\lambda_\theta = \inf_N \lambda_\theta(N)$$

as the smallest attainable average normalized length for any source blocklength.

Shannon's variable-length source coding theorem relates λ_θ to the entropy of the source when the source θ is known in advance:

Theorem 2.1 (Shannon): Given a source θ ,

$$N^{-1} H(X^N/\theta) \leq \lambda_\theta (N) < N^{-1} H(X^N/\theta) + N^{-1} \tag{2.1}$$

where

$$H(X^N/\theta) \triangleq E_\theta \{-\log \mu_\theta^N (X^N)\}$$

is the Nth-order entropy of the source θ (or the conditional entropy of the class of sources given θ). All logarithms are to the base 2. If the source is stationary, then

$$\lambda_\theta = H(X/\theta) \tag{2.2}$$

where $H(X/\theta) = \lim_{N\to\infty} N^{-1}H(X^N/\theta)$ is the entropy rate of the source θ.

An optimal code C_N for a given N can be constructed so that

$$-\log \mu_\theta^N (x^N) \leq N\ell (x^N | C_N) < - \log \mu_\theta^N (x^N) + 1 \tag{2.3}$$

Note that the construction satisfies (2.1) but requires advance knowledge of the source θ for which the code is to be constructed.

A useful performance index of any code C_N used on a source θ is the difference between the actual resulting normalized average length and the optimal attainable for that blocklength. We formalize this quantity as the redundancy or conditional redundancy given θ, r_θ (C_N), given by

$$r_\theta (C_N) \triangleq \ell_\theta (C_N) - \lambda_\theta (N) . \tag{2.4}$$

This definition is slightly different than that usually used [6] of $r'_\theta(C_N) = \ell_\theta (C_N) - N^{-1} H(X^N/\theta)$ which compares the average redundancy of a particular code with a possibly unachievable (except in the limit) lower bound. We use (2.4) here because we feel it is a more realistic comparison, results in a closer analogy with the figures of merit of later sections, and because the asymptotic $N \to \infty$ results are unaffected through (2.2) for stationary sources. Clearly $0 \leq r_\theta (C_N) \leqq r'_\theta (C_N)$.

We now consider the more general situation of coding for a class of sources, i.e., we must now choose a code C_N without knowledge of the actual source, θ, being observed. A sequence of these codes $\{C_N\}_{N=1}^{\infty}$ will be said to be universal in accordance with the definition of Section I if these codes designed without knowledge of θ asymptotically perform as well as optimal codes custom designed for the true (but unknown) θ, i.e., if $r_\theta (C_N) \underset{N\to\infty}{\to} 0$ in some sense regardless of θ. The various types of universal codes will correspond to the various notions of convergence, e.g., convergence in measure, pointwise convergence and uniform convergence.

Before formalizing these concepts, it is useful to consider in some detail a specific simple example to hopefully make believable the remarkable fact that such universal codes exist and to provide a typical construction.

Suppose that the class Λ consists of all Bernoulli processes, i.e., all independent, identically distributed sequences of binary random variables. The sources in the class are uniquely specified as noted in Section (I,B) by $\theta = \Pr[X_n = 1]$, i.e.,

$$\mu_\theta^1 (x_1) = \theta^{x_1} (1-\theta)^{1-x_1}, \quad x_1 = 0,1$$

$$\mu_\theta^N (x^N) = \prod_{i=1}^{N} \theta^{x_i} (1-\theta)^{1-x_i} = \theta^{w(x^n)} (1-\theta)^{N-w(x^n)} \tag{2.5}$$

where $w(x^n) = \sum_{i=1}^{n} x_i$ is the Hamming weight of the binary n-tuple x^n.

Choosing a code C_N to minimize $r_\theta (C_N)$ for a particular θ will clearly result in a large redundancy for some other sources. To account for the entire class we instead proceed as follows: Each source word x^N is encoded into a codeword consisting of two parts. The first part of the codeword is $w(x^N)$, the number of ones in x^N. This specification requires at most $\log(N+1)$ bits. The second part of the codeword gives the location of the $w(x^N)$ ones by indexing the $\binom{N}{w(x^N)}$ possible location patterns given $w(x^N)$. Thus this information can be optimally encoded (given $w(x^N)$) using equal length codewords of at most $\log \binom{N}{w(x^N)} + 1$ bits.

If the actual unknown source is θ , the resulting redundancy using this uniquely decodable code is bounded above as follows:

$$r_\theta(C_N) \leqq N^{-1}\left(\log(N+1) + 1 + E_\theta\left[\log\binom{N}{w(x^N)}\right] + 1 - \lambda_\theta(N)\right).$$

The $N^{-1}(\log(N+1)+2)$ term clearly vanishes as $N\to\infty$. Using Stirling's approximation and the ergodic theorem.

$$N^{-1}\log\binom{N}{w(x^N)} = N^{-1}\log\frac{N!}{w(x^N)!\,(N-w(x^N))!}$$

$$\underset{N\to\infty}{\to} -\frac{w(x^N)}{N}\log\frac{w(x^N)}{N} - \frac{N-w(x^N)}{N}\log\left(\frac{N-w(x^N)}{N}\right)$$

$$\underset{w.p.1}{\to} -\theta\log\theta - (1-\theta)\log(1-\theta)$$

The last step also follows from the strong law of large numbers (a special case of the ergodic theorem, $N^{-1}w(x^N)\underset{N\to\infty}{\to}\theta$ w.p. 1) and the continuity of the logarithm. From the Shannon theorem, $\lambda_\theta(N)\underset{N\to\infty}{\to}H(X/\theta) = -\theta\log\theta - (1-\theta)\log(1-\theta)$ so that $r_\theta(C_N)\to 0$ for all θ and the given sequence of codes.

We now proceed to the general definitions of universal codes and the corresponding existence theorems.

Given a probability measure on Λ (and an appropriate σ-field), a sequence of codes $\{C_N\}_{N=1}^{\infty}$ is said to be weighted-universal (or Bayes universal) if $r_\theta(C_N)$ converges to 0 in W-measure, i.e., if

$$\lim_{N\to\infty}\int_\Lambda dW(\theta)\,r_\theta(C_N) = 0 \tag{2.6}$$

The sequence is maximin-universal if (2.6) holds for all possible W. The measure W might be a prior probability or a preference weighting. The sequence is said to be weakly-minimax universal (or weakly-universal) if $r_\theta(C_N)\to 0$ pointwise, i.e.,

$$\lim_{N\to\infty} r_\theta(C_N) = 0\,, \quad \text{all } \theta\in\Lambda \tag{2.7}$$

The sequence is said to be strongly-minimax universal or minimax-universal or strongly-universal if $r_\theta(C_N) \to 0$ uniformly in θ, i.e.,

$$\lim_{N\to\infty} r_\theta(C_N) = 0 \text{ , uniformly in } \theta. \tag{2.8}$$

The types of universal codes are analogous to the types of optimal estimates in statistics.

Uniform convergence is the strongest and practically most useful type since it is equivalent to the following: Given an $\epsilon > 0$, there is an N_ϵ (not a function of θ) such that if $N \geq N_\epsilon$, then

$$r_\theta(C_N) \leq \epsilon \text{ , all } \theta.$$

The advantage here is that a single finite blocklength code has redundancy less than ϵ for all θ.

A strongly-minimax universal sequence of codes is obviously also weakly-minimax. Since $r_\theta(C_N) \geq 0$, weakly-minimax code sequences are also weighted universal for any prior by a standard theorem of integration. Since $r_\theta(C_N) \geq 0$, convergence in measure implies convergence W-almost everywhere (with W-probability one). Thus, if $\{C_N\}$ is a weighted universal sequence for Λ, then there is a set Λ_0 such that $W(\Lambda - \Lambda_0) = 0$ and $\{C_N\}$ is a weakly-minimax universal sequence for the class of sources Λ_0. Since convergence W-a.e. implies almost-uniform convergence, given any $\epsilon > 0$, there is a set Λ_ϵ such that $W(\Lambda - \Lambda_\epsilon) \leq \epsilon$ and $\{C_N\}$ is a strongly-minimax universal sequence for Λ_ϵ.

Even though the strongly-minimax universal codes are the most desirable, the weaker types are usually more easily demonstrated and provide a class of good code sequences which can be searched for the stronger types. The following theorem is useful in this regard:

Theorem 2.2: Given a discrete alphabet A, weighted-universal codes exist for the class of all finite entropy stationary ergodic sources with alphabet A and any weighting W that is a probability measure.

Proof: Let μ denote the average or mixture measure induced by W and the μ_θ, i.e., $\mu^N(x^N) = \int_\Lambda dW(\theta)\mu_\theta^N(x^N)$. This measure is clearly stationary and hence application of Shannon's theorem to the mixture measure yields for each

N a code C_N such that

$$\ell(C_N) = E\{\ell(X^N | C_N)\} \leq N^{-1} H(X^N) + N^{-1}$$

where $H(X^N)$ is the Nth order entropy of the mixture source. Thus for these codes

$$\begin{aligned}\int_\Lambda r_\theta (C_N) dW(\theta) &\leq \int_\Lambda dW(\theta)\{E_\theta\{\ell(X^N|C_N)\} - \lambda_\theta(N)\} \\ &= E\{\ell(X^N|C_N)\} - \int_\Lambda dW(\theta)\lambda_\theta(N) \\ &\leq N^{-1} H(X^N) + N^{-1} - N^{-1}\int_\Lambda dW(\theta) H(X^N|\theta) \\ &= N^{-1}\{H(X^N) - H(X^N|Ⓗ)\} + N^{-1} \\ &= N^{-1} I(X^N; Ⓗ) + N^{-1}\end{aligned}$$

where $I(X^N; Ⓗ)$ is the average mutual information between the unknown source index and the output N-tuples. In [5] it is shown for the class considered that $N^{-1} I(X^N; Ⓗ) \to 0$ as $N \to \infty$, completing the proof. This convergence to zero follows since the source outputs of an ergodic source eventually uniquely specify the source in the limit and therefore the per-letter average mutual information tends to zero. The theorem can also be proved by construction [6].

Using the ergodic decomposition, the above theorem can be extended to the apparently more general class of all stationary processes.

Unfortunately, existence theorems for weakly-minimax and strongly minimax universal codes are not as easily obtainable. As an alternative approach, the following theorem (proved in [6]) provides a construction often yielding universal codes for certain classes of sources.

Theorem 2.3: Codebook Theorem. Let $\{\Gamma_j ; j = 1,\dots,J_N\}$ be a partition of the source N-tuple output space with "representatives" $\theta_1, \dots, \theta_{J_N}$. Let j(.) be the mapping of x^N into the index of the Γ_j^N containing it, i.e., $x^N \in \Gamma_{j(x^N)}$. If for all θ there are vanishing sequences $\epsilon_\theta(N) \geq 0, \delta_\theta(N) \geq 0$

and a measure μ^N not depending on θ, such that

$$E_\theta \left[N^{-1} \log \frac{\mu_\theta^N (X^N)}{\mu^N_{\theta_{j(X^N)}} (X^N)} \right] \leqslant \epsilon_\theta (N)$$

$$E_\theta \left[-N^{-1} \log \mu^N \left(\Gamma_{j(X^N)} \right) \right] \leqslant \delta_\theta (N)$$

then weakly-minimax universal codes exist. If ϵ_θ (N) and δ_θ (N) do not depend on θ, then strongly-minimax universal codes exist.

Code constructions follow immediately whenever the codebook theorem applies. Make a codebook on the source output space for each of the representative values θ_j. Send the codeword in two parts. The first part consists of the value $j(\underline{x}_N)$ encoded with a word of length $-\log \mu^N [\Gamma_{j(x^N)}] + 1$. The second part consists of the codeword for $\underline{x}_N$ in the $j(x^N)$th codebook.

As an example of the application of the codebook theorem, consider the binary sources of eqn. (2.5). The representative values are $\theta_j = j/N$, $j = 0,1, \ldots, N$. $\Gamma_j = \{\underline{x}_N : \text{Hamming weight } j\}$. $\mu^N(\Gamma_j) = (N+1)^{-1}$.
Obviously

$$E_\theta \left[N^{-1} \log \frac{\mu_\theta^N (X^N)}{\mu_\theta^N \left(X^N | \theta_{j(X^N)} \right)} \right] =$$

$$E_\theta \left[N^{-1} \log \frac{\theta^{j(X^N)} (1-\theta)^{N-j(X^N)}}{\left(\frac{j(X^N)}{N} \right)^{j(X^N)} \left(1 - \frac{j(X^N)}{N} \right)^{N-j(X^N)}} \right] \leqslant \epsilon(N) = 0$$

$$E_\theta \left[-N^{-1} \log \mu^N (\Gamma_j) \right] \leqslant \delta(N) = \frac{\log(N+1)}{N} .$$

The codebook theorem can be used to solve many other coding problems. Suppose for any fixed θ, the source is stationary and ergodic. The source is then called conditionally stationary ergodic. The following theorem can be proven:

Theorem 2.4: For any conditionally stationary ergodic source, weighted universal codes exist. If there exists a probability function, $q(x_1)$, such that

$$E\,[-\log q(X_1)\,|\theta] < \infty \,, \tag{2.9}$$

for every $\theta \in \Lambda$, then weighted universal codes exist. If the supremun of (2.9) is finite over Λ and there exists a vanishing sequence $\{\epsilon_k\}$ such that for all N, M $\geq$ k, all $\theta \in \Lambda$.

$$N^{-1} H(X^N|\theta) - M^{-1} H(X^M|\theta) < \epsilon_k, \tag{2.10}$$

Then minimax universal codes exist.

Theorem 2.4 is established by the codebook theorem where the representative values $\{\theta_j\}$ are k^{th} order Markov source values which can be taken by a source histogram. As $N \to \infty$, $k \to \infty$ in such a way that (2.10) is satisfied.

III. Fixed-Rate Noiseless Coding

In some application variable length coding is not allowed. Instead, for some rate R one must encode each source block of length N into a fixed length coded representation of RN bits. Assuming that there are more than 2^{RN} possible message blocks, there will be some nonzero probability of error associated with this operation. For "noiseless" coding we would like to know how big R must be so that vanishing probability of error can be assured by choosing N large enough. In direct analogy to Section II, weighted, maximin, minimax and weakly minimax universal codes can be defined over a source parametrized by a random variable Ⓗ on a space Λ, with performance measured by error probability rather than redundancy. For conditionally stationary ergodic sources, the results of Section II can be combined with the law of large numbers (as used in the McMillan asymptotic equipartition property) to obtain the following theorem:

Theorem 3: For encoding any conditionally stationary ergodic source, if $R > \lim_{N\to\infty} \sup_{\theta \in \Lambda} N^{-1} H(X^N \mid \theta)$, weighted and weakly minimax universal codes exist.

IV. Universal Coding on Video Data

The idea of variable length universal coding was applied to a recorded satellite picture of the earth consisting of 2400 lines, each line containing 4096 8 bit samples. The sample-to-sample differences, $\{x_i\}$, were formed and modeled as having the probability mass function:

$$\mu_\theta(x_i) = \frac{1-\theta}{1+\theta}\,\theta^{|x_i|} \tag{4.1}$$

It is well known that this is a reasonable approximation for video data. From (4.1) and the independence assumption,

$$\mu_\theta^N(\underline{x}_N) = \left(\frac{1-\theta}{1+\theta}\right)^N \theta^{\sum_{i=1}^{N} |x_i|} \tag{4.2}$$

Choosing representative values of θ, five codebooks were generated - one fixed length PCM coder, three variable length coders on the individual $\{x_i\}$, and one run length coder. As indicated by the codebook theorem, each block was encoded by each of the five codebooks with the shortest codeword chosen for the actual representation with a prefix code added to denote the codebook. The resulting average rate was three bits per sample at a block size of $N = 64$. For increasing or decreasing block sizes about this value, the rate was found to increase slowly. For larger blocksizes the nonstationarity of the data causes the increase, whereas for smaller blocksizes, the prefix "overhead" information causes the increase. As a basis for comparison, the actual sample entropy of the differences was calculated and found to be 3.30 bits per sample across the picture. Note that this is the minimum that any of the usual coding schemes can achieve. The universal coding scheme can do better than the entropy, in apparent contradiction to the usual source coding theorem, by taking advantage of the non-stationary nature of the source.

V. Fixed-Rate Coding Subject to a Fidelity Criterion

We now drop the requirement of a perfect reproduction and require only that some average fidelity constraint be satisfied. Thus compression is now attainable by eliminating unnecessary precision as well as redundancy. Let $\hat{A}$ be an available reproducing alphabet, i.e., the possible letters in the compressed reproduction. Usually, but not necessarily $\hat{A} \subseteq A$, e.g., the result of quantizing. Let $\rho(x,y)$ be a nonnegative distortion measure defined on $A \times \hat{A}$, i.e., for all $x \in A, y \in \hat{A}$. The distortion between N-tuples is assumed to be single-letter, i.e.,

$$\rho_N(x^N, y^N) \triangleq N^{-1} \sum_{i=1}^{N} \rho(x_i, y_i) .$$

A codebook C_N is a collection of $\| C_N \| < \infty$ codewords or N-tuples with entries in $\hat{A}$. A source x^N is encoded using C_N by mapping it into the best codeword in the ρ_N sense, i.e., into the $y^N \in C_N$ minimizing $\rho_N(x^N, y^N)$. The resulting is denoted $\hat{x}(x^N)$. The codebook together with the encoding rule is called a code and is also denoted by C_N. If the code C_N is used on a source θ, the parameters of interest are the rate of the code

$$R(C_N) = N^{-1} \log \| C_N \|$$

and the average distortion resulting from using C_N on θ

$$\rho_\theta(C_N) = E_\theta[\rho_N(X^N | C_N)]$$

where

$$\begin{aligned} \rho_N(x^N | C_N) &= \rho_N(x^N, \hat{x}(x^N)) \\ &= \min_{y^N \in C_N} \rho_N(x^N, y^N) . \end{aligned}$$

Compression is achieved since the code size $\| C_N \|$ is usually much smaller than the number of possible source N-tuples (which is in general uncountably infinite) and hence any codeword can be specified by using fewer bits than the original source required. (Strictly speaking, "compression" is achieved if $R(C_N) \leqslant H(X)$, the entropy rate of the source). Fidelity is lost as a result of the compression, but the goal is to minimize this hopefully tolerable loss. The optimal performance is now specified by the minimum attainable average distortion using fixed rate codes. The rate may be constrained by channel capacity, available equipment, receiver limitations, storage media, etc. Let $\mathcal{C}(N,R,\hat{A})$ be the class of alphabet $\hat{A}$, blocklength N codes having rate less than or equal to R. Define

$$\delta_\theta(R,N,\hat{A}) = \inf_{C_N \in \mathcal{C}(N,R,A)} \rho_\theta(C_N)$$

$$\delta_\theta(R,\hat{A}) = \inf_N \delta_\theta(R,N,\hat{A})$$

δ_θ parallels the λ_θ performance measure of noiseless coding. It can be shown [10] that if θ is stationary, then the limit of $\delta_\theta(R, N, \hat{A})$ exists and equals the infimum over N. Shannon's theorem on source coding with a fidelity criterion relates the desired optimal δ_θ to a well-defined information theoretic minimization called the distortion-rate function (DRF). This theorem is important since δ_θ (like λ_θ) cannot in general be directly evaluated while the DRF is amenable to fast computer computation via nonlinear programming techniques [11].

The DRF of a stationary source θ with available reproducing alphabet is defined by

$$D_\theta(R,\hat{A}) = \lim_{N\to\infty} D_\theta(R,\hat{A},N)$$

$$D_\theta(R,\hat{A},N) = \inf_{N^{-1} I(X^N,\hat{X}^N) \leq R} E_\theta\{\rho_N(X^N,\hat{X}^N)\}$$

where the inf is over all test channels (conditional probability measures for $\hat{X}^N$ given X^N, random encoders) and $I(X^N,\hat{X}^N)$ is the average mutual information between input and output N-tuples of the given source and test channel [12,13].

Theorem 5.1: (Shannon, Gallager, Berger). Given a stationary ergodic source θ, if there exists a reference reproduction letter a* such that

$$E_\theta\{\rho(X^1,a^*)\} < \infty$$

then

$$\delta_\theta (R,\hat{A}) = D_\theta (R,\hat{A})$$

Theorem 5.1 resembles Theorem 2.1 in that it relates optimal performance to an information theoretic quantity. Unlike Theorem 2.1, however, Theorem 5.1 only relates these quantities asymptotically, i.e., there is no general relation between δ_θ $(R,\hat{A},N)$ and D_θ $(R,\hat{A},N)$. Analogous to redundancy in the noiseless case, define the discrepancy of a rate R code C_N as the difference between actual performance for the given class of codes:

$$d_\theta (C_N) = \rho_\theta (C_N) - \delta_\theta (R,\hat{A},N)$$

We next consider source coding for a class of sources. A sequence of codes $\{C_N\}_{N=1}^{\infty}$ will be said to be universal if d_θ $(C_N) \rightarrow 0$ in some sense for all θ. The various types of universal fixed rate codes with a fidelity criterion are defined by the type of convergence exactly as in the noiseless case. The comparisons and relative strengths are obvious generalizations of the noiseless case.

Given a probability measure W on Λ, a sequence of codes $\{C_N\}$ is said to be weighted-universal if

(5.1)
$$\lim_{N\to\infty} \int_\Lambda dW(\theta) d_\theta (C_N) = 0 ,$$

weakly-minimax universal if

(5.2.)
$$\lim_{N\to\infty} d_\theta (C_N) = 0, \text{ all } \theta \in \Lambda$$

and strongly-minimax universal if

(5.3)
$$\lim_{N\to\infty} d_\theta (C_N) = 0 , \text{ uniformly in } \theta .$$

Before proceeding to the general case, we consider as before a nearly trivial case to make the existence of such codes believable and to demonstrate a typical construction.

Theorem 5.2: Strongly-minimax (and therefore weakly-minimax and weighted) universal codes exist for any finite class of stationary sources.

Proof: Say the class contains K sources $k = 1,\ldots,K$. $\delta_k(R,\hat{A})$ can be shown to be a continuous function of R so that given an $\epsilon > 0$ there exists an N sufficiently large to ensure that for all k

$$|\delta_k(R-N^{-1}\log K,\hat{A},N) - \delta_k(R,\hat{A})| \leqq \epsilon/2$$

For each source k build a nearly optimal blocklength N code $C_N(k)$ of rate $R-N^{-1}\log K$ such that

$$\rho_k(C_N(k)) \leqslant \delta_k(R-N^{-1}\log K,\hat{A},N) + \epsilon/2$$

The extra $\epsilon/2$ is necessary since a code actually yielding the infimum defining δ_k may not exist. Form the union codebook $C_N = \bigcup_{k=1}^{K} C_N(k)$ containing all the distinct codewords in all of the subcodes $C_N(k)$. The encoding rule is unchanged, i.e., a source block is encoded into the best codeword in C_N. Since this word can be no worse than the best word in any subcode $C_N(k)$, the average distortion resulting from using C_N on the source k satisfies

$$\begin{aligned}\rho_k(C_N) &\leqslant \rho_k(C_N(k))\\ &\leqq \rho_k(R-N^{-1}\log K,\hat{A},N) + \epsilon/2\\ &\leqq \rho_k(R,\hat{A}) + \epsilon\end{aligned}$$

The rate of C_N is given by

$$\begin{aligned}R(C_N) &= N^{-1}\log \|C_N\|\\ &\leqq N^{-1}\log K \max_k \|C_N(k)\|\\ &\leqq N^{-1}\log K + (R-N^{-1}\log K) = R\end{aligned}$$

completing the proof.

The basic idea is that with a slight decrease in rate (that asymptotically vanishes), we can build a code that accounts for all possibilities by combining subcodes for each possible source.

The finite case does not generalize immediately as in general there are an uncountably infinite class of sources and we cannot possibly build a subcode for each. If, however, the class can be partitioned into a finite number of subclasses such that sources within a subclass are "similar" or "close" in some way in that a code designed for a single representative of the subclass works "well" for all members of the subclass, then the resulting subcodes can be combined as previously to obtain a universal code sequence. With differing definitions of "similar" and "well", this topological approach has resulted in the most general known existence theorems for weakly and strongly-minimax universal codes. An example of this approach will be presented in the proof of the strongly-minimax universal coding theorem which, unlike the noiseless case, is here the easiest to demonstrate.

We now proceed to statements of the various universal coding theorems. The required technical assumptions are given for completeness.

Theorem 5.3: Weighted-Universal Coding Theorem [4,8,14]

Given a metric distortion measure ρ on $(A \cup \hat{A}) \times (A \cup \hat{A})$ such that A is a separable metric space under ρ and every bounded set of $\hat{A}$ is totally bounded, let Λ be the class of all ergodic alphabet A processes. If there is a reference source letter a^* such that

$$E_\theta\{\rho(X^1, a^*)\} < \infty, \quad \text{all} \quad \theta \in \Lambda$$

and if for the weighting W, $\int_\Lambda dW(\theta)\, E_\theta\, \{\rho(X^1, a^*)\} < \infty$, then weighted-universal codes exist for Λ.

The theorem follows directly from the source coding theorem for stationary nonergodic sources [4] as generalized in [14] since a mixture of ergodic sources is equivalent to a single stationary source for which there exists a sequence $\{C_N\}$ such that

$$\lim_{N\to\infty} \rho(C_N) = \lim_{N\to\infty} E\{\rho(X^N|C_N)\}$$
$$= \lim_{N\to\infty} \int_\Lambda dW(\theta) E_\theta \{\rho(X^N|C_N)\}$$
$$= \int_\Lambda D_\theta(R,\hat{A})dW(\theta) = \int \delta_\theta(R,\hat{A})dW(\theta)$$

yielding the theorem [8]. The proof of the source coding theorem used is a complicated generalization of random coding arguments and a topological decomposition of Λ using the ergodic decomposition.

The distortion measure ρ is defined on $(A\cup\hat{A}) \times (A\cup\hat{A})$ as the above theorem is proved using a two-step encoding combining the regular encoding with a quantization within the source or reproduction alphabet. Hence distortion must be defined on $A\times A$ and $\hat{A}\times\hat{A}$ as well as $A\times\hat{A}$.

The previous theorem is conceptually easily generalized to classes of stationary sources using the ergodic decomposition. Numerous technical measurability problems arise, however, and such results are more easily obtainable using the following theorems.

Theorem 5.3: Weakly-Minimax Universal Coding Theorem [8,10].

Given a metric distortion measure ρ on $(A\cup\hat{A}) \times (A\cup\hat{A})$ under which either A or $\hat{A}$ is a separable metric space, then weakly-minimax universal codes exist for the class of all stationary processes with alphabet A. When A is separable, the theorem is proved using the previously described topological approach of carving up the class of sources [8]. The distance used is the distribution or variational distance. When $\hat{A}$ is separable, the method of proof is a generalization of Ziv's combinatoric proof [8,10] that does not involve the structure of the source class, but attempts to fit a given code structure as well as possible to whatever source block is observed.

In [8] this theorem is proved first for special simple cases and then for the general cases where the topological and combinatoric approaches are compared and contrasted in some detail. Instead of further considering the details of weakly-minimax universal codes, however, we proceed to a discussion of strongly-minimax universal codes as these are practically the most useful type, the proof is easy and demonstrates the basic topological approach. In addition, an interim step in the proof provides an interesting side result giving a measure of the mismatch occurring when applying a code designed for one source to another.

To state the theorem in its most general form, we require the concept of the $\bar{\rho}$ distance between random processes and a simple application. Given two stationary processes θ and ϕ, the $\bar{\rho}$ distance $\bar{\rho}\,(\theta,\phi)$ is defined by

$$\bar{\rho}\;(\theta,\phi) \;=\; \sup_n \bar{\rho}_n\,(\theta,\phi)$$

$$\bar{\rho}_n\,(\theta,\phi) \;=\; \inf_{q\in Q_n(\theta,\phi)} E_q[\rho_n\,(X^n,Y^n)]$$

where $Q_n(\theta,\phi)$ is the class of all joint distributions q describing random vectors (X^n, Y^n) such that the marginal distributions specifying X^n and Y^n are μ_θ^n and μ_ϕ^n, respectively. Thus $\bar{\rho}_n$ measures how well X^n and Y^n can be matched in the ρ_n sense by probabilistically connecting the random vectors in a way consistent with their given distributions. Alternative definitions and properties of the $\bar{\rho}$ distance are given in [7] and [8] . In particular, it is there proved that $\bar{\rho}$ is a metric and that $\bar{\rho}$ has the following simple (but less useful here) alternative definition:

$$\bar{\rho}(\theta,\phi) \;=\; \inf_{\{W_n\}_{n=-\infty}^{\infty}} E(\rho(X_0,Y_0))$$

where $\{W_n\}_{n=-\infty}^{\infty}$ are stationary random processes of pairs $W_n = (X_n, Y_n)$ such that the coordinate process $\{X_n\}$ is the θ process and $\{Y_n\}$ is the ϕ process. Thus $\bar{\rho}$ measures how well the processes can fit together in the $\bar{\rho}$ sense at a single time if the processes are stochastically linked in a jointly stationary manner. The usefulness of $\bar{\rho}$ is demonstrated by the following simple and intuitive theorem:

Theorem 5.4: Mismatch Theorem
For any blocklength N and any codebook C_N,

$$|\rho_\theta(C_N) - \rho_\phi(C_N)| \leq \bar{\rho}(\theta,\phi) \quad .$$

Proof: Let q nearly yield $\bar{\rho}_n$, i.e., $E_q[\rho_n\ (X^n,Y^n)] \leq \bar{\rho}_n\,(\theta,\phi)+\epsilon$. If θ describes (X^n,Y^n), then X^n and Y^n are distributed according to μ_θ^n and μ_ϕ^n, respectively, so that we have from the triangle inequality that

$$\rho_\theta(C_N) = E_\theta\{\rho(X^N | C_N)\}$$

$$= E_q\{\rho(X^N | C_N)\}$$

$$= E_q\{\inf_{z^n \in C_N} \rho(X^N, z^N)\}$$

$$\leqq E_q\{\inf_{z^N \in C_N} \{\rho(X^N, Y^N) + \rho(Y^N, z^N)\}\}$$

$$\leqq \bar{\rho}_n(\theta, \phi) + \epsilon + E_q\{\rho(Y^N | C_N)\}$$

$$\leqq \bar{\rho}(\theta, \phi) + \epsilon + \rho_\phi(C_N)$$

Since ϵ is arbitrary, reversing the roles of θ and ϕ completes the proof.

Using optimal codes in the above theorem immediately yields the following:

Corollary:

$$|\delta_\theta(R, \hat{A}, N) - \delta_\phi(R, \hat{A}, N)| \leqslant \bar{\rho}(\theta, \phi) \quad \text{all} \quad N$$

and, therefore, if the sources are ergodic

$$|D_\theta(R, \hat{A}) - D_\phi(R, \hat{A})| \leqslant \bar{\rho}(\theta, \phi).$$

Theorem 5.4: Strongly-Minimax Universal Coding Theorem

If the class Λ is totally bounded under $\bar{\rho}$, i.e., if given $\epsilon > 0$ there is a finite partition $\{B_k\}_{k=1}^{K}$ where $K = K(\epsilon)$ of Λ such that if θ, $\phi \in B_k$, then $\bar{\rho}(\theta, \phi) \leqslant \epsilon$, then there exist strongly-minimax universal codes for Λ.

Proof: For each set B_k in the partition, let k be a representative source, i.e., k indexes any fixed θ in B_k. Construct as in Theorem 5.1 a universal code C_N for the finite class of sources k = 1, ..., K. Application of this code to Λ yields the following: Given a source θ, it must lie in some subclass B_k in the partition, say $B_{k(\theta)}$. We have from the proof of Theorem 5.2 and the above construction that

$$\rho(C_N|\theta) \leq \rho\,(C_N|k(\theta)) + \bar{\rho}(\theta,k(\theta))$$

$$\leq \delta_{k(\theta)}(R,\hat{A}) + \epsilon(2 + \bar{\rho}(\theta,k(\theta))$$

$$\leq \delta_\theta(R,\hat{A}) + \epsilon(2 + 2\bar{\rho}(\theta,k(\theta))$$

$$\leq \delta_\theta(R,\hat{A}) + 5\epsilon/2$$

$$R(C_N) = R$$

completing the proof.

Intuitively, to build a strong-minimax code we "cover" the class by a finite number of "representative" subcodes that together have rate R. Each subcode works nearly optimally for a subclass of the class.

An example of a totally bounded class of sources under $\bar{\rho}$ is the class of all stationary finite-state wide-sense Markov chains of order less than some finite integer. Extensions to more general classes along with partial converses may be found in [8].

In practice one might reverse the order of construction by first choosing a reasonable number, K, of representative subcodes and of rate R and blocklength N with resulting rate $R + N^{-1} \log K$ and average distortion within $\epsilon(K)$ of the optimal. An appropriate choice of blocklength will allow use of this construction on nonstationary sources that are locally stationary [15].

VI. Variable-Rate Coding with Distortion

The average distortion of the encoding at a fixed rate as in the last section depends upon the actual value of θ in effect, that is, the actual stationary ergodic source seen by the encoder. Thus distortion is a random variable over the ensemble with distribution given by the distribution of the parameter θ. In many applications it may be more desirable to allow the coding rate to depend on θ while holding the average distortion fixed over the ensemble.

As in the last section, a coding theorem will be established for the special case of a finite number of subsources, $\theta = 1,2...,K$, in the ensemble. As before, the theorem holds for noncountable ensembles as well, but the proof is considerably more involved. In addition, it will be assumed that there is a maximum distortion value, ρ_M.

For each value of k, generate a set of codewords according to the usual coding theorem for stationary, ergodic sources. If $R_k(D)$ is the rate distortion function in bits of the kth subsource, and D is the desired value of average distortion, each code will contain L_k codewords where

$$\log L_k = (N(R_k(D-\epsilon) + \epsilon). \tag{6.1}$$

ϵ is an arbitrary positive constant and the blocksize is chosen large enough so that the average distortion is $D - \epsilon$ for all θ and so that the probability that there is no codeword with distortion less than $D - \epsilon/2$ is less than $\epsilon/2\rho_M$.

The coded representation of each of the L_k codewords generated for each k will consist of two parts. The first part will be the fixed length binary number equal to k-1, $k = 1,2....,K$ using at most $\log K + 1$ bits to identify the codeword. The second part will be the location of the codeword in a list for each k of length at most $\log L_k + 1$ bits. Thus the rate of any codeword for a given θ is at most

$$r_k = \frac{\log K + 2}{N} + R_k(D-\epsilon) + \epsilon \text{ bits}. \tag{6.2}$$

Obviously by choosing N large enough and ϵ small enough, the rate can be made arbitrarily close to $R_\theta(D)$ for $\theta = 1,2,...,K$.

The achievement of D and $R_\theta(D)$ for the combined supercode depends upon the actual choice of a codeword out of the $L = \sum_{i=1}^{K} L_j$ codewords total. The coding rule is as follows. Upon observing an output block of length N, among the codewords of distortion less than D - $\epsilon/2$, find the one of minimum rate, if any. If there is no codeword with distortion less than D - $\epsilon/2$, make a random choice. The average rate for θ = k then

$$\leqslant r_k + (\sup_j r_j) \text{ Prob}\begin{bmatrix}\text{no codeword of distortion} \\ \text{less than D in the } t^{th} \text{ code}\end{bmatrix}$$

$$\leqslant r_k + (\sup_j r_j)\, \epsilon/2\, \rho_M \tag{6.3}$$

$$= \frac{\ell n\, M + 2}{N} + R_k(D - \epsilon) + \epsilon + (\sup_j r_j)\, \epsilon/2\rho_M \,,$$

which is abritrarily close to R_k (D) for small enough ϵ, large enough N. The average distortion for $\theta = k$ is

$$\leqslant D - \epsilon/2 + \rho_M \text{ Prob}\begin{bmatrix}\text{no codeword of distortion} \\ \text{less than D in the } k^{th} \text{ code}\end{bmatrix}$$

$$\leqslant D - \epsilon/2 + \rho_M \epsilon/2\rho_M = D.$$

Further details can be found in [9].

VII. Conclusions

We have summarized a unified formulation of source coding--both noiseless and with a fidelity criterion-- in inaccurately or incompletely specified statistical environments. Several alternative definitions of universally good coding algorithms have been presented, the most general known existence theorems stated, and proofs given for some simple informative cases. The results indicate that surprisingly good performance is possible in such situations and suggest possible design philosophies, i.e., (1) estimate the source present and transmit both estimate and an optimal codeword for the given estimate source, or (2) build several representative subcodes and send the best word produced by any of them. In the first approach, asymptotically the estimate well approximates the true source and takes up a negligible percentage of the codeword. In the second approach, if the representatives are well chosen, all possible sources are nearly optimally encoded with an asymptotically negligible increase in rate.

The results described are largely existence theorems and therefore do not prescribe a specific method of synthesizing data compression systems. They do, however, provide figures of merit and optimal performance bounds that can serve as an absolute yardstick for comparison justification for overall design philosophies that have proved useful in practice.

REFERENCES

[1] SHANNON, C.E., "The Mathematical Theory of Communication", University of Illinois Press, 1949, Urbana, Illinois.

[2] _____,"Coding Theorems for a Discrete Source with a Fidelity Criterion", in IRE Nat.Conv.Rec., pt. 4, pp. 142-163, 1959.

[3] ROZANOV, YU., "Stationary Random Processes", Holden-Day, San Francisco, 1967.

[4] GRAY, R.M., and DAVISSON, L.D., "Source Coding Theorems without the Ergodic Assumption", IEEE Trans. IT, July 1974.

[5] GRAY, R.M., and DAVISSON, L.D., "The Ergodic Decomposition of Discrete Stationary Sources", IEEE Trans. IT, September 1974.

[6] DAVISSON, L.D., "Universal Noiseless Coding", IEEE Trans. Inform. Theory, Vol. IT-19, pp. 783-795, November 1973.

[7] GRAY, R.M., NEUHOFF, D., and SHIELDS, P., "A Generalization of Ornstein's d Metric with Applications to Information Theory", Annals of Probability (to be published).

[8] NEUHOFF, D., GRAY, R.M. and DAVISSON, L.D., "Fixed Rate Universal Source Coding with a Fidelity Criterion", submitted to IEEE Trans. IT.

[9] PURSLEY, M.B., "Coding Theorems for Non-Ergodic Sources and Sources with Unknown Parameters", USC Technical Report, February 1974.

[10] ZIV, J., "Coding of Sources with Unknown Statistics-Part I: Probability of Encoding Error; Part II: Distortion Relative to a Fidelity Criterion", IEEE Trans.Info.Theo., vol IT-18, No. 4, July 1972, pp. 460-473.

[11] BLAHUT, R.E., "Computation of Channel Capacity and Rate-Distortion Functions", IEEE Trans.Info.Theo., Vol. IT-18, No. 4, July 1972, pp. 460-473.

[12] GALLAGER, R.G., "Information Theory and Reliable Communication", New York, Wiley, 1968, ch. 9.

[13] BERGER, T., "Rate Distortion Theory: A Mathematical Basis for Data Compression", Englewood Cliffs, New Jersey, Prentice-Hall.

[14] NEUHOFF, D., Ph.D. Research, Stanford University, 1973.

[15] GRAY, R.M., and DAVISSON, L.D. "A Mathematical Theory of Data Compression (?)", USCEE Report, September 1974.

CONTENTS

RATE DISTORTION THEORY AND DATA COMPRESSION

By T. Berger

UNIVERSAL SOURCE CODING

By Lee D. Davisson

Printed in the United States
By Bookmasters